PRAISE FOR
THE CHURCH CAN GO TO HELL

"I guarantee you that this book will shock you, inspire you, and bless you. The one thing it will not do is allow you to remain unchanged."

KEITH GILES
Author of the Best-Selling *"Jesus Un"* Book Series

"This jaw dropping, tell-all book will have you wanting to read more! There is something shared in every chapter you can either relate to or maybe even bear witness to. I am excited about what the Lord will do through this real, raw and uncut testimony. This book is destined to inspire, encourage and set a nation of people *free* from the bondage of what has happened to them in the past and may even be happening now. This is truly *a must read* by all!

STEPHANIA "MZ. JAZZY" PRIESTER
The Jazzy Report

"Tears. Beautifully written. OMG … Desimber has encapsulated everything that my heart and mind has wanted to say to the church all these years."

DREEK DOWNS
Bedroom Kandi Lifestyle Consultant

"In this book, Desimber Rose breaks down every barrier that stands in the way of mankind knowing God in an authentic way. This book exposes all the man-made falsities about the gospel of Jesus Christ, and she makes herself relatable to everyone who has been mishandled by church culture through her authentic and transparent approach in telling her raw and uncut testimony. Once you pick this book up you won't be able to put it down!"

PASTOR VINCENT HENDERSON
The Freedom Agency Counseling & Coaching Services LLC

"Wow! I'm absolutely flabbergasted by Desimber's boldness to spread the truth. It's definitely time. I'm claiming bestseller not because of how the book was written but by the conviction that one will feel as they dig deeper within themselves. There is so much content that it will be hard to digest, but if an individual isn't convicted in any form by reading this book, then it's definitely not for them. Walls will be torn down as a result of her transparency, and hearts will be broken, which is what we know as conviction. *Hearts need to be broken!* If this is the case, know that she's done her job."

KORTNEY A. DAVIDSON, PSY.D; PH.D.
Xhale Meditation Services, LLC

"I barely know what to say about this book. Not because it's not fantastic—it *is* that—but because it's so good that any words of praise I give it will not suffice. But be forewarned! It will kick your ass. From the very first line to the final paragraph, it is relentless—in the best of ways. Give *The Church Can Go to Hell* a read and be ready for a challenge, because in being challenged, that's where you will discover growth."

MATTHEW J. DISTEFANO
Author of multiple books, cohost of the Heretic Happy Hour podcast, and long-time social worker

THE CHURCH CAN GO TO HELL

OVERCOMING THE BROKENNESS, BITTERNESS, AND BONDAGE OF CHURCH HURT

DESIMBER ROSE WATTLETON

Copyright © 2022 by Desimber Rose Wattleton

Second Edition

Cover design and layout by Rafael Polendo (polendo.net)
Cover image by Marcus Grip (shutterstock.com)

WARNING: This entire book is a trigger. Enter in at your own risk.

DISCLAIMERS: Some names and identifying details have been changed to protect the privacy of individuals. I have tried to recreate events, locales and conversations from my memories of them. In order to maintain their anonymity in some instances I have changed or omitted the names of individuals and places, I may have changed some identifying characteristics and details such as physical properties, occupations and places of residence. The facts and theories presented here are based upon the author's personal experience, understanding, and interpretation of events, scripture, and human behavior. Although the author and publisher have made every effort to ensure that the information in this book was correct at press time, the author and publisher do not assume and hereby disclaim any liability to any party for any loss, damage, or disruption caused by errors or omissions, whether such errors or omissions result from negligence, accident, or any other cause.

This is *my* testimony and interpretation thereof, if you happen to be one of the people involved in any event described in this book and have an alternative interpretation or perspective based on your experience you are welcome to write and publish a book accordingly.

ISBN 978-1-957007-16-8

This volume is printed on acid free paper and meets ANSI Z39.48 standards.
Printed in the United States of America

 QUOIR

Published by Quoir
Oak Glen, California
www.quoir.com

This book is dedicated to The Church.

Every time we use religion
to draw a line to keep people out,
Jesus is with the people
on the other side of that line.

HUGH L. HOLLOWELL

TABLE OF CONTENTS

FOREWORD
BY JOANNE MCAFEE MALDONADO

The thief does not come except to steal, and to kill, and to destroy. I have come that they may have life, and that they may have it more abundantly.
JOHN 10:10 (NKJV)

People who have trauma are attracted to religion. Let me say that again. People who have trauma are attracted to religion.

Trauma comes from the sense of powerlessness in the midst of surprising or painful experiences. We don't know which end is up and we don't trust anyone. Not even ourselves. We already believe we are not worthy of love or good things in life. Trauma actually grooms us to be really good, compliant religious people.

Religion offers a God who agrees you're unworthy and there's nothing good in you but one who will tell you what to think and how to behave. It also offers you membership into a large group who will also agree that you're unworthy and deserving of hell but who you can celebrate with because you've followed what religion taught you will save you from yourself, from continuing to be unworthy, and from eternal conscious torment.

It's a savior that uses your brokenness to mold you into the likeness of all the others while selling the idea that this is what God wants.

You'll believe you're an individual with special gifts that can be used in the elite kingdom built by religion but you will not be allowed to deviate from the ways you are taught or ever question the foundational "truths" by which your circles operate. You cannot think for yourself. Your life choices, such as your mate, your job, when and where you buy a home, when and where you are allowed to minister to others will all be out of your control and submitted to the "covering" you're taught you need to function.

If you feel ready to deal with your trauma, you will be encouraged to ignore it and adopt the belief that it's disappeared because you are part of the flock. This will continue to hinder you from true healing and functioning in life from a place of wholeness. This will keep you dependent on all I've already mentioned.

I love Jesus with all my heart and I have a relationship with him, but the Jesus I know and understand from scripture came to free people from religion. He constantly says, "it is written" or "you have heard" and names mindsets that people were taught … But counters it by saying, "but I tell you …" He paid with his life to show humanity that they are made in the likeness and image of the Creator and he's crazy about them. Jesus purposely pursued those the religious saw as corrupt and unsavable to prove there is no separation between God and man. It's a destructive rumor.

Religion is not the life more abundant. It's another very large chain masquerading as freedom. In my experience, which is all I can truly speak from, I could never have experienced healing and freedom while practicing religion. They are one another's complete opposite.

I pray we all experience healing and freedom in this lifetime.

INTRODUCTION
BY JESUS CHRIST

These are the Words of Christ, quoted verbatim, as written in The Holy Bible in Matthew Chapter 23:1-33. (NLT)

"The teachers of religious law and the Pharisees are the official interpreters of the law of Moses. So, practice and obey whatever they tell you, but don't follow their example. For they don't practice what they teach. They crush people with unbearable religious demands and never lift a finger to ease the burden.

Everything they do is for show. On their arms they wear extra wide prayer boxes with Scripture verses inside, and they wear robes with extra-long tassels. And they love to sit at the head table at banquets and in the seats of honor in the synagogues. They love to receive respectful greetings as they walk in the marketplaces, and to be called 'Rabbi'.

Don't let anyone call you 'Rabbi,' for you have only one teacher, and all of you are equal as brothers and sisters. And don't address anyone here on earth as 'Father,' for only God in heaven is your Father. And don't let anyone call you 'Teacher,' for you have only one teacher, the Messiah. The greatest among you must be a servant. But those who exalt themselves will be humbled, and those who humble themselves will be exalted.

What sorrow awaits you teachers of religious law and you Pharisees. Hypocrites! For you shut the door of the Kingdom of Heaven in people's faces. You won't go in yourselves, and you don't let others enter either.

What sorrow awaits you teachers of religious law and you Pharisees. Hypocrites! For you cross land and sea to make one convert, and then you turn that person into twice the child of hell you yourselves are!

Blind guides! What sorrow awaits you! For you say that it means nothing to swear 'by God's Temple,' but that it is binding to swear 'by the gold in the Temple.' Blind fools! Which is more important—the gold or the Temple that makes the gold sacred? And you say that to swear 'by the altar' is not binding, but to swear 'by the gifts on the altar' is binding. How blind! For which is more important—the gift on the altar or the altar that makes the gift sacred? When you swear 'by the altar,' you are swearing by it and by everything on it. And when you swear 'by the Temple,' you are swearing by it and by God, who lives in it. And when you swear 'by heaven,' you are swearing by the throne of God and by God, who sits on the throne.

What sorrow awaits you teachers of religious law and you Pharisees. Hypocrites! For you are careful to tithe even the tiniest income from your herb gardens, but you ignore the more important aspects of the law—justice, mercy, and faith. You should tithe, yes, but do not neglect the more important things. Blind guides! You strain your water so you won't accidentally swallow a gnat, but you swallow a camel!

What sorrow awaits you teachers of religious law and you Pharisees. Hypocrites! For you are so careful to clean the outside of the cup and the dish, but inside you are filthy—full of greed and self-indulgence!

You blind Pharisee! First wash the inside of the cup and the dish, and then the outside will become clean, too.

What sorrow awaits you teachers of religious law and you Pharisees. Hypocrites! For you are like whitewashed tombs—beautiful on the outside but filled on the inside with dead people's bones and all sorts of impurity. Outwardly you look like righteous people, but inwardly your hearts are filled with hypocrisy and lawlessness.

What sorrow awaits you teachers of religious law and you Pharisees. Hypocrites! For you build tombs for the prophets your ancestors killed, and you decorate the monuments of the godly people your ancestors destroyed.

Then you say, 'If we had lived in the days of our ancestors, we would never have joined them in killing the prophets.' But in saying that, you testify against yourselves that you are indeed the descendants of those who murdered the prophets. Go ahead and finish what your ancestors started.

Snakes! Sons of vipers! How will you escape the judgment of hell?"

*Can you grieve with me
over what religion has done
to the simplicity of Christ?*

DR. DAVID JEREMIAH

CHAPTER 1
SHOTS FIRED

BROKEN

"Damn. I'm all the way in the back of you girl." And he was. All. The. Way. Back. Back when I noticed I was the darkest of my mother's children. Back when my father sent me my first bike from prison at 5 years old. Back when my first boyfriend broke up with me. I could keep going back, but the point is I never left. This is that sinking moment when you realize you're not as grown as you thought … that this was never about you … that you've gone too far but feel powerless to turn around…trapped. Something in me needed to be loved so deeply that I was willing to give myself away in exchange for what I thought was love.

So here I am, 18 years old, on my back in the backseat of my pastor's car, losing my virginity. It hurt, but not like I thought it would. It hurt my soul, and I didn't even know what a soul was until then. I woke up, from a dream within a dream, consciously unconscious. It's almost like I ate from the tree of knowledge of good and evil. Because at that moment, when he said those words, I immediately became aware of the difference between lust and love. Not that I even knew what love was, but whatever love was, I knew this wasn't it. He asked if I was ok, and I said "Yes." We both knew I wasn't. I felt my hymen break that night, and I've been broken ever since.

We drove back from the dark place he took me in almost complete silence. Everything in me screaming how stupid I was, how evil I was, how dumb I was to think that this was anything more than just a man, being a man. Crazy thing is, I loved his wife, like a mother. But somehow, I managed to compartmentalize myself as her daughter, and his lover.

She knew. She looked at me in church with both pity and pain. She knew I was old enough to know better, but he was to blame. She heard the extra compliments; she saw the lingered hugs. She knew before I did, that I was the one. She watched, and she waited. Could she accuse him of something he had not yet done? I guess not. More importantly, did she really want to stop this from happening? Because the truth is, I was the perfect storm. She wanted out, and he wanted in.

She was a model first lady—beautiful, graceful, and gifted. She could cook, sing, direct the choir, and teach Sunday School. And like so many first ladies she was faithful to a man she no longer loved. She regretted marrying him, she resented the day she made those vows, and she longed for an opportunity to do it all over again. Because she knew, and he knew, if they had it to do over, they wouldn't. In public she praised him, she honored him, she loved him. In private she despised him, she loathed him. She was trapped. I guess you could say I freed them both.

It only happened once, but that was enough. He owned me after that. I will never forget one Sunday, I decided I just didn't feel like going. Everyone knew but no one was saying anything. I didn't feel like being the elephant in the room. I didn't go to church that Sunday. My phone is blowing up. He's calling me and I won't answer. After ignoring his calls all day, I finally answered the phone. "Where were you?" … "Why weren't you at church today?" … "You don't know how much I need you!" … Try to keep in mind that I'm 18 years old, senior year in high school, friends with his stepdaughter, and used to be something like a daughter to his wife. And here I am now, being checked by a man who felt like he owned me enough to dictate to me that I owed him my presence in church, because somehow it made him feel better when I was there. Again, he asked, "are you okay?" He actually seemed concerned. I said yes, again. We both knew I wasn't. I was trying to hold on to my life, to myself, but I was losing, I was losing everything.

Fast forward to graduation day, I somehow managed to get through the school year, but not without wiping out everything I worked for academically up to that point. Once a 4.0 model student, my GPA was now hovering just over 2.5, but I made it. This moment was bittersweet. I should've been celebrating with my friends. Instead, my family was congratulating me less than 15 feet from my Pastor, First Lady, and their daughter, my friend. But we couldn't celebrate together, because by that time everyone knew. It felt like the whole town knew.

Later that evening I remember going to the senior graduation party at El Papagayo's. She was there, my friend. We tried to enjoy ourselves, but there was so much space between us. We were in the same room, on the same dance floor, but worlds apart. I remember hugging her, and saying in her ear, loudly over the music, "remember no matter what happens, I love you." We hugged each other and cried a little bit, then went back to dancing like everything was normal. I think we both knew we'd never see each other again. She probably doesn't even remember this … but I remember every second of my life back then.

The following Monday, I packed up what little things I owned, and moved from my hometown in Moses Lake, to my dad's house in Seattle, Washington.

IF THE TRUTH BE TOLD

The truth of the matter is I was set up by the Church. And the sad part about it is, I'm just one of many. Right now, in churches all across the world, from the storefronts to the cathedrals, some girl or boy, some vulnerable, broken young lady, and yes, even young man, is being groomed by a pastor or person in leadership. Instead of protecting them they are preying on them, patiently waiting for their opportunity to take something they were never entitled to. Waiting, watching, plotting and planning to manipulate their access to the souls entrusted to them.

I am not an anomaly; I am par for the course in a global religious institution that calls itself the Church but mirrors the world in every aspect of its structure and function. It doesn't matter if you go to a Pentecostal Holiness Church, an Episcopal Church, an Apostolic Church, a Catholic Church, a Baptist Church, a COGIC Church, a Non-Denominational Church or whatever sect, cult, or creed of Church you claim, all of them are guilty. All of them protect positions and titles, while covering up the men and women behind them, and in doing so subject their members to emotional, mental, spiritual, and physical abuse.[1]

Churches would rather keep up a public front in the midst of a scandal than address, root out, and destroy the perpetrator of the scandal. And in their effort to keep up the façade, they make the victim the scapegoat. The fact that you told someone, the fact that you reached out for help, the fact that it happened to you becomes the scandal, and the victim becomes the outcast while they respect and restore the "Mand of God" (and yes I spelled that word like that on purpose). If you grew up in the "bapticostolic" churches I grew up in, then you recognize this over-emphasized pronunciation of folks attempting to "sound holy."

I remember going to one of the church mothers for counsel following the fallout when everything became public. I will never forget what she said, "I knew he was going to get somebody ... it was either going to be you or Stacy." And on top of that she laughed about it like it was funny ... it was surreal. I just remembered thinking, wow, this is all a joke to everyone, just one more piece of gossip, just another day in the church, but my whole entire life was falling apart. And here she was, a church mother, laughing and talking about how she "knew this was going to happen."

Think about that for a moment. How many times have people sat idly by, watching from the sidelines, as their leader becomes a predator and actively pursues the sheep as prey? How many are reading this

---

1   For example, the recent revelations regarding sexual abuse cover-up by the Southern Baptist Convention: https://www.washingtonpost.com/religion/2021/06/05/russell-moore-southern-baptist-sex-abuse-allegations/

book right now and have been a witness to a church covering up the wicked behavior of the pastor, from the first lady down to the deacons, everyone just waiting and watching as the pastor devours the church? It sounds unreal, but it's happening Every Single Day in the Body of Christ! People are watching their leaders lie, cheat, steal, and manipulate the Church with their mouths closed. Why? Perhaps it's because they're in the inner circle, and they don't have the courage or the liberty to speak out against it because they're part of it. It's hard to confront wrongdoing if you have to confess you're part of the problem.

We come to church broken, vulnerable, and in need of healing only to be used as bait by the enemy. And we ask ourselves, how did I get here? How did this happen? I don't know about anyone else, but as for me, I needed a father! I needed a father's voice. I needed the affirmation of a father. I needed the comfort and protection of a father. I didn't meet my father until I was 8 years old. Up until that time he was in prison. He was a drug dealer in Seattle, and he spent much of his life in and out of the penitentiary. Now he was the best father he had the capacity to be and anything I asked in my adult life he always answered the call. But he was the product of an abusive childhood, growing up on the streets in Chicago, born and raised in an abusive environment. His mother was brutally abused by his father. She died from alcoholism when he was just 14 years old, and his father died in prison. He loved me beyond measure, and I knew it, but it usually showed up in the form of the latest tennis shoes, name brand clothes, and electronics. He tried to give me what he didn't have materially coming up, but he couldn't give me what he didn't have emotionally.

On the flip side, my mom was a single mother to 5 children, a strict disciplinarian who taught us how to survive, and the meaning of hard work and integrity, but struggled in the nurturing department. She also grew up in an abusive environment, raised by an alcoholic, abusive mother. To top it off she was raped multiple times and sexually abused by my grandmother's husband and male friends. When she told my grandmother, she didn't believe her, and instead despised her. I wonder how many young ladies are dealing with this right now in the Body of Christ … but at the hands of their pastor, youth leader, or some other person who's supposed to be protecting them?

My mother ran away from home at the age of 13 and raised herself on the streets. So, she did the best she could, she taught us what she knew, and that was how to survive. She taught us that we didn't need anybody to make it. At this point in her life she has made amends with her past, and we've had long, meaningful conversations that have brought healing to the broken places over the years. But, the truth of the matter is we do need someone to make it. We all need someone. And many of us search for that sense of belonging and that voice of affirmation in the Church.

We come to the Church broken, with any number of generational weights holding us down, seeking to be lifted with love, acceptance, and direction. Instead, too often we find the exact opposite— judgment, rejection, and confusion. I needed the voice of The Father. Instead, I was groomed by a man who acted like a father figure, but was a wolf in sheep's clothing, just waiting for me to become legal enough to violate. And the church watched it happen. All over the world right now, the church is watching it happen. And when the darkness finally comes to light, the victims are blamed for their own demise. Was I grown? According to the laws governing the State of

Washington, yes. Did I consent, yes. But the bigger question is, why did he ask?

After 4 years of deposits there was no way he wasn't going to take a withdrawal at some point—with interest. Every compliment, every gift, every meal, every word of encouragement, every smile, every pat on the back—and lower when no one was looking—every inappropriately long hug, was an investment. And I paid the dividends with my body, my integrity, and my innocence. He gave me what my father didn't, but he never loved me like a father, taking something sacred from me was always the objective.

The trick of the enemy is to make you believe you owe it to someone to allow them to violate you. To make you believe it's what *you* want, until you're there, naked and exposed, with all your dignity on the floor, trying to figure out what just happened. Trying to explain that yes you consented but it's not what you wanted, but you didn't know it wasn't what you wanted, you only knew what you needed, but didn't realize this wasn't it, until it was done. But by that time, you're the slut … the one "they always knew was fast" … the homewrecker, the one who ruined the church. And he? Well, he's the Pastor, the Man of God, and we shouldn't judge. We just need to pray, and we all make mistakes, and that's between him and his wife, and we got the Church Anniversary next Sunday. Who's bringing the potato salad?

The truth is they were all miserable. She was never about that First Lady life. That was his calling, not hers. And if she's honest with herself, I'm the best thing that ever happened to her. I was the bridge too far, I was the straw that broke the camel's back, I was her "biblical reason" for divorce. I was her justification. I was her ticket out of a failed marriage to a man she stopped loving long before they ever showed up at that church.

A few years after the incident happened, I came home to visit, and my mother informed me that his wife had called and asked to meet with me. She wanted to tell me that she had forgiven me, that she knew I didn't pursue her husband. Although I was relieved to receive this act of kindness, it was apparent to me that this was less something she was giving to me and more something she was giving herself. She needed closure. But I can't help but wonder, had she ever forgiven herself? Had she ever forgiven herself for watching and waiting, while he was watching and waiting? Had she ever forgiven herself for ignoring how he was treating me? Did she ever forgive herself for not protecting me from him? Did she ever forgive herself for hoping and praying that one day he would do the unthinkable so the church wouldn't judge her for divorcing him? Had she ever forgiven herself for playing the role of a model first lady with resentment, regret, and disgust in her heart?

She was trapped in her own religious convictions with a man she couldn't stand; getting up Sunday after Sunday after Sunday to put on a show. She saw me coming. She saw all of us. I just happened to be the one he chose. And she knew it. But I don't suppose she could sound the alarm, could she? Because if she did, then she would have to acknowledge that she married a pedophile. I wonder if she ever forgave herself for letting me be the reason. Because the bottom line is, I wasn't. If the truth be told, I was the one who rescued her.

F*CK THE CHURCH

They say gifts and callings are without repentance. Thank God they aren't without judgment. Because if we had to wait on the church to take sexual abuse seriously, we'd be waiting a long time. A Religious

News Service article published on January 9, 2014 details the story of a Memphis pastor arrested for sexually abusing a 16-year-old family member. What makes this heartbreaking story even more repugnant is that church and family members had been informed about the abuse two years earlier but failed to report the crime to the police. Instead, they decided that the best response was to simply pray for the offender and hope for the best. Tragically, this response to child sexual abuse by those within the church is not uncommon. Equally as tragic is that such responses fuel perpetrators to continue destroying the bodies and souls of untold numbers of children.

Let me tell you something: Hoping and Praying is never the proper response to sexual abuse! It's the equivalent of seeing 27 souls murdered at Sandy Hook Elementary and responding with "thoughts and prayers" instead of enacting common-sense gun reform. It sounds nice, but it means nothing to the families who must go on without their loved ones, and it will inevitably happen again. Are you hoping and praying the abuser will stop, like somehow, they will hear from heaven and turn from their wicked ways? Or are you hoping and praying the victim will be able to withstand your twisted, wicked version of the Gospel that somehow suggests they should keep quietly complicit as loyal prey while you protect the predator? There is no justification for this, and yet it's justified every day, Sunday to Sunday, as abusers are allowed back into the pulpit after their "mistake", allowed to teach children, lead youth departments, and counsel vulnerable adults reaching out for wholeness only to be broken in the hands of repeat offenders.

We like to make the Catholic Church the red-headed stepchild of sexual abuse. But the truth of the matter is no denomination is exempt. Every one of them have systems in place that enable, empower, and encourage the abuse of the congregation at the hands of those in leadership.

The numbers don't lie. In her book, *Predators, Pedophiles, Rapists, and other Sex Offenders,* author and clinical psychologist Anna Salter highlights multiple studies that expose the magnitude of these events. An *Abel Harlow Child Molestation Prevention Study* found there were more than 291,000 incidents attributed to 561 sexual offenders, and only 3% of the offenders had a chance of being caught. Dr. Salter reveals in her book that of the sexual offenders interviewed, they admitted to penetrating between 10 to 1250 victims. She wrote that every offender was previously reported by the children, and those reports were ignored.

On February 10, 2019, *The Houston Chronicle* published an investigative report covering 20 years and 700 victims of sexual abuse in the Southern Baptist organization of churches. Journalists in the two newsrooms spent more than six months reviewing thousands of pages of court, prison and police records and conducting hundreds of interviews. They built a database of former leaders in Southern Baptist churches who have been convicted of sex crimes. This is what the investigation revealed:

- At least 35 church pastors, employees and volunteers who exhibited predatory behavior were still able to find jobs at churches during the past two decades. In some cases, church leaders apparently failed to alert law enforcement about complaints or to warn other congregations about allegations of misconduct.

- Several past presidents and prominent leaders of the Southern Baptist Convention are among those criticized by victims for concealing or mishandling abuse complaints within their own churches or seminaries.

- Some registered sex offenders returned to the pulpit. Others remain there, including a Houston preacher who sexually assaulted a teenager and now is the principal officer of a Houston nonprofit that works with student organizations, federal records show. Its name: Touching the Future Today Inc.

- Many of the victims were adolescents who were molested, sent explicit photos or texts, exposed to pornography, photographed nude, or repeatedly raped by youth pastors. Some victims as young as 3 were molested or raped inside pastors' studies and Sunday school classrooms. A few were adults—women and men who sought pastoral guidance and instead say they were seduced or sexually assaulted.

David Pittman, victim of molestation by a youth minister at the age of 12, summed it up best. "So many people's faith is murdered. I mean, their faith is slaughtered by these predators." Not too quick to forgive those who prayed but took no action, Pittman said "That is the greatest tragedy of all" ... having confessed that after almost 40 years, he only recently stopped hating God.

Pittman is just one of countless others who translate their experience with the church as Acts of God. And it makes sense, right? Because the church is supposed to be a representative of the nature of God, yet everywhere you look, on any given Sunday, what you find time and time again, is principalities, powers, rulers of the darkness of this world, and spiritual wickedness in high places.

If this is what it's going to be … if all the church has to offer is predators, pedophiles, and perverts … if this is what we should expect, if this is it, let me be the first to say, with the utmost conviction and sincerity, fuck the church.

Still here? Good. I just needed to let that sit with you for a second … to validate how we've all felt at one point or another if we're honest. Also, I need to sift out the hyper-religious, ultra-legalistic, holier than thou, super saints. Because anybody I lost on the last page isn't ready for this book. Like Jack Nicholson said in *A Few Good Men*, "You can't handle the truth!" But you're still here, so that means not only can you handle it, you're ready for it, and more importantly, you need it.

To answer the question on the last page, *this is not it.* God's Church has so much more to offer than predators, pedophiles, and perverts. It's just that if you're looking for his Church in buildings, conferences, revivals, and organized religion, it may be hard to find. But I can tell you with unwavering conviction and sincerity, God is real, so is his Church, and both are worth seeking.

It is one thing to lose people you love.
It is another to lose yourself.
That is a greater loss.

DONNA GODDARD, WALDMEER

CHAPTER 2
LOST AND FOUND

STARTING OVER

Seattle, Washington. 18 years old, starting over before I even started my life to begin with. I moved in with my dad, and it was different. For the first time I was on my own. He was still dealing drugs, still about that life. I was trying to make sense of the world, trying to find direction. I became a workaholic … I'm still a workaholic. I was working in the daytime for CityYear as an AmeriCorps volunteer. And at night I was working third shift at a manufacturing plant in Kent. I was pulling 16-hour days.

One night I was driving home from my third shift job, coming down the highway from Kent to Tukwila, and I fell asleep. I don't know how long I was asleep, I just know I ended up on the other side of a 5-lane highway and when I woke up I was driving straight, with no traffic beside me on either side … God has always had his hand on my life. I barely made it home, but not before dozing off again and nearly taking out a mailbox right before the turn to my dad's house. That was the last time I went to that job. Work was my drug of choice … is my drug of choice.

I felt lost. I needed a church home, I needed to feel grounded, I needed to be fed. I don't remember who invited me, or how I became a member. But, at some point I started attending King of Glory Tabernacle COGIC in Renton, Washington. I was in the choir, I was a youth leader, I was the director of the step team. I finally felt like I belonged. I felt like this is where I needed to be. The word was awesome, the people were nice, and I was growing, spiritually. Then, one day I'm at choir rehearsal, on stage, and in walks the pastor ... no, not The Pastor ... but *my* pastor, the one from Moses Lake. I couldn't believe it, how did he find me?! Of all the churches in the Greater Seattle area, this man walks into this one. I felt like someone was playing a cruel trick on me. He saw me, I started crying and one of the sisters stepped outside with me. I told her this was the man who used to be my pastor, and gave her a few details about the situation, of course she was shocked and asked me what he was doing there; I told her I didn't know.

I calmed down, went back inside, and finished rehearsal. He came up to me afterward and asked if he could talk to me, I said, "No, what are you doing here? How did you even find me?!" He told me to calm down, he had no idea I would be there. He told me he had just moved to the area and that he was taking on the janitorial contract for the school side of the church. He said his friend's wife was the principal of the school and he had helped him get the cleaning contract, that he had no idea that he would run into me. He asked if he could talk to me. I said no. He begged me, and finally, I said yes. I told him I would meet him at IHOP at 10:00pm because I had something to do.

Around midnight, I still hadn't decided if I was going to meet him or not. Finally, I went, thinking he wouldn't be there, and this would all be over. But, surprisingly, he was sitting there, at almost 1:00am, waiting for me. I told him I was just there to listen and go on my way. He began with an apology. He told me he was now divorced, that things fell apart at the church, and that he moved in with his friend in the Seattle area, hoping to start over.

He kept apologizing … he told me he loved me; I didn't believe it … but I wanted to. I wanted all of this to make sense. I wanted to believe it was fate that found me at choir rehearsal that night. I wanted to believe God had something to do with this. He kept talking. I kept listening … until I was in his bed again. He was the only man I had ever been with sexually.

How in the world could I feel safe in the arms of a predator? No matter how angry I thought I was, apparently the door was only closed, not locked. I still responded to his voice. I still wanted to be loved. I still needed to be affirmed. I still yearned for the voice of The Father. So, this is what a soul-tie is … a spiritual gateway to the soul accompanied by physical manifestations. There is nothing inherently evil about a soul-tie, aside from the motive and intent of the person who has access to the gate. Which begs the question put so unforgettably by the Right Reverend B.W. Smith, "Who in hell left the gate open?" And the answer to that question, is me. When you don't take intentional measures to heal from trauma, you leave the gate open. When you just "get over it" but don't overcome it, you leave the gate open. When you try to pursue your future without reconciling your past, you leave the gate open.

He asked me 7 times, I said No 6 times … even my soul knew better. But I reached out for counsel, and I'll never forget what the pastor said to me, "you might as well marry him, you done already ruined his life." All the while he was laughing … I laughed in return, not because it was comical, but that uneasy laugh when you don't know how to respond.

His words dropped like an anvil on my chest. Wow ... somehow, I ruined his life, a man who groomed me from the age of 14, prophesied to me, spoke life to me, took the place of my father, then manipulated me into being his lover at just past legal. These words, from a Pastor, affirmed everything negative I felt and thought about myself. It was my fault. I did destroy his marriage. I disappointed the church and my family. I am the reason this happened to me. Feeling broken and obligated, I said yes, the 7th time. And there I was, 19 years old, less than a year out of high school, married to my 35-year-old pastor, who had his eyes ... and his hands ... on me since I was 14 years old.

We got married at St. James C.M.E., his friend's church, where he was the minister of music. We barely had a wedding to speak of, I wore my prom dress, and we got a cake from the grocery store. Less than 15 people were in attendance. My father refused to come. My mother tried her best to be supportive. But everyone knew I was making a mistake, even I knew it. But I felt indebted to him, and I was desperate for my life to make sense ... for it to be all part of "God's Plan". So here I am, married at 19 years old, to the same man who groomed me 5 years earlier at the age of 14. I didn't know anything about life, or the world, or what it meant to be a wife. All I had was my faith and my convictions, I was a blank slate for him to write upon.

He introduced me to gambling, apparently this was a vice of his. It was exciting, when you won. But devastating when you lost. It was a rollercoaster ... my whole life was a rollercoaster. We moved several times, he never held down a job more than a few months. I tried to go back to college a few times, searching for some kind of accomplishment, some way back to the girl I was before that night in the backseat of his car. We moved several times, we could never keep the rent paid, we were never stable. We finally moved to a nice house in Tacoma, which was owned by the Pastor of the new church we were attending. He had managed to get another gig as minister of music, and the pastor was trying to help us, he was a good man. He gave me a job at the church daycare, I started working with the youth again, and things seemed like they might actually be ok. But it didn't last long.

Once again, I found myself on my back. Except this time his hands are around my neck, choking me on the living room floor of our home. Apparently, I had committed the cardinal sin of confronting him about something he did that I believed was unthinkable. At just 20 years old I was now the primary bread winner, working as a legal secretary for the Law Office of Grant & Grant in Tacoma, Washington.

One day before I left for work, I gave my husband the money to pay the rent, which was already late. Before I could get home from work, I received a phone call from the landlord asking when he should expect the rent, my heart dropped. I confronted him when I got home, apparently, he had gambled away the rent money, and also drained my bank account.

It never ceases to amaze me how angry people can get when you confront them with what they did wrong to you. Nevertheless, here I am, gasping for breath, and somehow, I managed to muster the strength to speak, barely a whisper, but he heard me loud and clear … "If you don't kill me, I'm going to kill you." He jumped up and told me I was crazy, but he didn't think I was serious. Gasping for breath I got to my feet as quickly as my strength began to return, grabbed the biggest knife from the kitchen I could find and began chasing him.

First all around the house then up the stairs, at some point I dropped the knife ... I don't know when or how, I was clearly out of it ... and the fight ensued, all I remember is pushing him down the stairs ... from there I just remember running down the sidewalk barefoot, chasing him, screaming. He ran to a payphone and called the police on me. Yes, at this point my husband, my pastor, was afraid of *me*.

Just about this time my cousin Timmie Ree is passing by, screeches to a halt, pulls up, jumps out frantically and asks me "Are you okay cousin!?" (If you know her, then you know she was ready and able to fight for me). It is absolutely evident; I am not ok. True to form, she says something to the nature of, "why you out here in the street lookin' crazy and pretty?!" I am totally delirious, I am screaming, I am crying, and I am threatening to kill the man that tried to kill me moments earlier ... and I believe I would have if I could've. These are the moments we should thank God for the grace that kept us. About this time the police arrive. We're both telling our side of the story, with bruises on both of us. We were both arrested for Criminal Domestic Violence. Yes, you read that right. Pastor Desimber Rose was arrested, charged, and booked into the Pierce County Jail in Tacoma, WA for a CDV, and still the Lord gave me favor.

I will never forget the officer who booked me in, he asked, what are you doing here? I was dressed for work, stockings ripped, barefoot, hair did, makeup smeared all over my face ... you could say I was beautiful and broken ... I didn't respond. He asked me, have you ever been to jail before? I said just above a whisper, "No." He walked me to the area where I had to strip down and put on an orange jumpsuit, then walked me to the holding area, and told the supervising officer, "take care of her, she doesn't belong here." They put me in a cell by myself, and I sat in jail that night, crying, trying to figure out how in the world I got there, but knowing, I didn't belong there. The next morning, we were taken before the judge, and I was informed I would be released, my husband didn't press charges against me … and he was released, because I didn't press charges against him.

So, here I am, walking home with the clothes I wore to work the day before, barefoot, ripped stockings. I heard him call out to me, I looked back, here comes my husband running to catch up to me, he gave me his shoes, we walked home, and he apologized. One of several apologies.

I stayed. I knew God hated divorce and my husband told me so. He knew I loved God, and he used the Word of God against me. On top of that, everyone in the church I confided in told me to stay … to pray. He convinced me I needed to move away from my family and that we needed a fresh start. so we packed up everything we owned and moved to Oakland, California. This was the beginning of the darkest years of my life.

I mentioned in the introduction that I'm writing this book in the middle of a global pandemic. All around the world domestic violence is spiking. For many the daily reprieve from their abusers during the work week has been erased. And now, a growing number of both men and women are sitting ducks, captive targets of the rage brewing inside their abusers. The pandemic did not create this wave of domestic abuse, it exposed the tectonic plates of unaddressed trauma constantly colliding with unchecked anger that have the tendency to be muted by our daily routines and desire to ignore the dysfunction of our own homes.

I will not say that this man constantly put his hands on me, but physical abuse is not the only kind of abuse inflicted on those too broken to begin again. Especially in the church, where more value is placed on the institution of marriage than the safety, well-being, and emotional, mental, and spiritual health of the individuals in the marriage.

There are countless women suffering abuse right now at the hands of their spouses, many of which attend church and even worse, hold positions in the church. The church has for centuries burdened women with the sins of men. For some reason, it always seems to be the woman's responsibility to "stay and pray" for years when most men wouldn't accept the same behavior for one day. It's called Toxic Patriarchy, and I'll deal with that a little later. But before I get back to California … My sister, my brother … yes, even men can be in abusive relationships. You don't deserve this. Love isn't supposed to hurt.

No matter what the church has told you, God is not requiring this of you. He loves you and would never subject his daughter or his son to abuse. More importantly, you are not alone. Church folks have perfected the art of presentation. You would be surprised how many come Sunday after Sunday, with smiles on their faces, shining like new money as the old folks say. And all the while there's pure hell at home.

FACING REJECTION

I was raised a Jehovah's Witness. One of the things I will never forget is having the door slammed in my face during field service. I can laugh about it now, but at the time it was humiliating. I was just 11 years old when it happened the first time. In training they tell you that you won't always be received but nothing can really prepare you for that kind of rejection, especially at just 11 years old. Add that to the fact that we were 1 of just 3 black families in the whole congregation. And it was easy to tell, even at 11 years old, that we were "different".

We attended the Kingdom Hall, but we were never really part of the body, I never felt like I belonged. The elders could hardly remember our names, and they would often confuse us with one of the other black families. Looking back as an adult, I guess you could say we were their "token blacks", you know the ones you can point to in order to claim you're a "multi-cultural" church. We had a few friends, some of which I've reconnected with over the years on Facebook, but never really felt like I was part of a church family. As a matter of fact, attending always felt like some kind of punishment.

I will never forget there was this one family, everything about them seemed so perfect, something like a modern-day Brady Bunch. And I kid you not, every single time I saw them they were dressed so nice, they seemed so happy, they were smiling, and as a kid I was in awe of them. I loved everything about them. They might as well have been celebrities as far as I was concerned.

I remember visiting their home for some kind of social function they were having for the kids and their house was so nice, it just seemed like their world was so perfect. Maybe it's because I was child, being raised by a single mother, barely making ends meet from month-to-month. Perhaps if I was an adult, I would've saw the signs, but I didn't. I can't remember how it came out, but I found out later that life for them was nothing at all as it appeared.

All I remember thinking is wow ... they looked so happy. And this is the problem with the church. Everyone is so busy "looking the part" and "playing their role" that few are actually living the part.

One of the many unfortunate dysfunctions covered up within the church is Domestic Abuse. An all too common reality hiding in plain sight from Sunday to Sunday all over the world. We see it, but we don't say anything … and if we do say something, it goes a little something like: "Pray for him. God is able to change his heart. You just have to have faith." Or some other nonsense that places the burden square upon the shoulders of the victim to intercede on behalf of their abuser while getting their mind, body, and soul dented by someone who has no meaningful relationship with God in the first place -and the proof is in how he or she is treating one of God's own. Author and Influencer, Jessica Ghigliotti, put it perfectly when she wrote about her own experience enduring abuse in the church, "God Hates Divorce—Abuse Is Fine."

According to the CDC, 1 in 4 women and 1 in 7 men will experience physical violence by their intimate partner at some point during their lifetimes. Think about that for a moment. As much as 1 in 4, and no less than 1 in 7 people in the church has experienced or is experiencing domestic violence right now. According to The Washington Post, domestic abuse leads to more than 30,000 deaths a year worldwide. I wonder how many of those who were killed by their spouse were counseled to "stay and pray" or guilted into believing that it was their duty to receive and withstand abuse at the hands of their husbands by their pastor or even elder women in their lives? Even one is one too many.

The Word of God should never be used to manipulate you into submission with guilt and fear. It is true that God hates divorce, but he loves you. And I believe that God hates for his children to live a defeated life of fear, brokenness, pain, trauma, low self-esteem and all the other manifestations of spiritual, physical, emotional, verbal, and financial abuse. You have no obligation to stay in a situation that is unsafe for you or your children, and detrimental to your mental and emotional well-being.

You are one decision away from a different life. You can do this. God loves you, and he will give you the strength, courage, wisdom, and provision to begin again. Trust God. Pray, Plan, and Pursuit your right to a life free from abuse, in all its forms. For more information about planning your exit and resources available in your area, please call the National Domestic Violence Hotline at (800) 799-7233.

AGAIN

Oakland, California. The biggest city I had ever lived in up to that point. We called ourselves starting over, but really, we just picked up where we left off. Once again, I was the primary breadwinner, working for a non-profit called Eureka Communities in Oakland. And just like before, his vice of gambling followed us, only I had become addicted to gambling as well by this time. It was nothing for me to get paid on Friday and blow an entire paycheck of $1,500 before noon the next day. We found ourselves homeless and living in a transitional home. Many times, I wanted to leave and come back home but pride wouldn't let me.

He was the minister of music for Cornerstone Missionary Baptist Church under the leadership of his cousin, Dr. Samuel Williams, Sr. I hardly spoke to anyone in the church. The people were nice enough, but since my husband was in leadership, I had a behind the scenes look at the ministry and I wanted nothing to do with it for the most part. I think it was about this time I really started hating the church. I don't think I ever resented God personally, but I came pretty close on multiple occasions. Even for a hardcore believer, it can be hard to separate the church and the people from God himself. The pastor and his wife were kind enough, but his "spiritual sons" were another matter entirely.

I will never forget a 3-day revival the church hosted one summer; the pastor had his spiritual sons each take a night. At the close of one of the revival all the preachers, with the exception of the pastor, decided to "go out" to San Francisco, and all the wives either went home or hung out at one of the pastor's homes until they got back. I don't know what I expected, I guess I thought they were going out to eat, maybe even have a few drinks, but what actually happened was so disgraceful I'm sure every one of them would deny it, never-the-less it's true. They "went out" to San Francisco and visited strip clubs. They came in after 1:00am loud and laughing like a bunch of college freshmen.

One of the men in this group was the same one who counseled me to "marry him, you done already messed up his life". I was sitting there at his home with his wife when they came back. Apparently, this kind of behavior was normal because his wife seemed unphased by the whole thing. They're going on and on about their exploits that evening and cracking on one of the preachers who apparently tried to hit on what he thought was a woman but turned out to be a transvestite. Again, I found myself laughing … one, because that part was actually funny … and two, because I couldn't believe this is what the pastors did after a freaking revival!

I wonder how often this happens. Probably more often than anyone would care to admit. You see these preachers in these pulpits, shouting the people, prophesying, laying hands on people, and their lives outside the church are more worldly than most of the "heathens" they claim to be trying to save.

At just 21 years old, I had a complicated, cynical view of the church. Everybody was suspect. I trusted no one, and I always defaulted to the worst-case scenario with just about all preachers. Even if they were kind, I was always trying to figure out what the angle was and what they would ask of me later.

Our time in Oakland didn't last long, just about long enough for my husband to borrow money from everybody he could and burn a bunch of bridges. One Sunday he told me it was our last Sunday and not to say anything about it to anyone. I told the first lady, she was always sweet to me, I gave her a hug and that was the last time I saw them.

So here we are, headed back to Washington and at this point it seems like I have no control over my life. My husband is almost 40 and I'm barely old enough to drink, so he's pretty much running the show. We landed in Pasco, which was something like the twilight zone. His ex-wife lived there, the old churches he used to preach and play at were there, I hardly knew anybody there, but I tried to act the part. Again, he became the minister of music at one of the churches. The pastor and his wife were kind, the people could sometimes be cliquish but for the most part it was another generic worship experience for me, at this point all churches were the same.

Of course, all our problems followed us, because you can change locations but unless you change yourself, it's going to be the same shit on a new day, in a new place, all over again. Gambling was still a problem, not so much for me but I was still an enabler. I kept thinking if I go with him, I could persuade him not to spend or lose so much money, it never worked. I tried to confide in a few people about what I was experiencing but somehow it got back to him. He convinced me I couldn't talk to anyone, that they all just wanted to be in our business, and it was making him look bad, etc. etc. etc.

I ended up being generally isolated, even from my own family … and that's how he liked it. I think it was about this time I actually started to hate him. I couldn't stand for him to touch me. I confided in one of the first ladies about it, and of course I was counseled not to withhold my body from my husband, because when we get married our bodies are no longer our own … blah blah blah. I know she meant well but fuck that logic! My body belongs to me. I don't owe it to any man to allow him entrance. Especially when he's treating me the way this man was treating me! That's what I thought to myself anyway. But I found myself looking up at the ceiling many times waiting for him to "finish" so I could go to sleep.

One time, I remember feeling so disgusted that after he came, I got straight out the bed, used the bathroom, and took a shower. He knew something was wrong, I remember him saying something like, are you trying not to get pregnant? Are you ok? Of course, I blew it off and said I was fine. We both knew I wasn't. I wasn't intentionally trying not to get pregnant; I was just trying to wash him off of me, I felt filthy. I never did get pregnant during this marriage; I hardly ever even had a menstrual cycle. Turns out I was under so much stress, it exasperated a condition I later found out was Polycystic Ovary Syndrome, and I had something called Amenorrhea. I went to the doctor a few times over the course of our marriage and was told I would either not be able to have children or that it would be very difficult to do so without fertility treatment. At the time it didn't bother me, I wasn't thrilled with the idea of being the mother of this man's children anyway.

He was very talented, he could preach, he could play, he could sing, and he could build just about anything from the ground up if he put his mind to it. Gifted people always have a problem holding down a job, and he was no exception. So, after he'd borrowed money from everyone he could, half-assed finished a few construction jobs, and burned his quota of bridges, it was time to move again.

Full circle, we find ourselves back in Moses Lake, the little town where it all happened. It was home, but it was such a strange place. Leaving as a high school graduate in the midst of a scandal in 1999, and coming back just 3 years later in 2002 as the wife of the Pastor who was introduced into my life at 14 years old was like being trapped in a twisted time warp of some kind. The only time I felt sane or happy was when I was with my family, and it seemed like he resented that, almost like he was jealous. We seemed to always have some kind of altercation when I spent time with my family … I'm sure he knew they didn't like him. They were always telling me I could do better, so I imagine that was part of his consternation.

The longer I was around my family, the more confident I became. It all came to a head one day. I don't remember what triggered it, but I had enough, and he knew it. I called my big sister to come pick me up. She was helping me pack my things to move out, at some point he rolled up on me like he was going to hit me, my sister got in his face and told him "I dare you, you better not put your hands on my sister nigga! You got the right one today!" (a little note from the back pew: if a black person ever tells you that you've "got the right one", you've in fact got the wrong one and you should deescalate that situation as expeditiously as possible). He just stood there looking powerless.

This time it was different. His reign over my life was over, and he knew it. I walked out of that house and left everything I owned. I left with a suitcase, a few clothes and a few pairs of shoes. I didn't have anything, and I didn't care, I was free ... for now.

My big sister had been in a bad car accident and was waiting on a settlement. She was going through a bunch of drama with her husband, too, at the time.

I hadn't been back home very long when she said one night, "let's leave, when I get this money let's just leave." I was like, "Bet, let's do it, but where are we going?" Our younger sister had moved down to South Carolina a few years before, so we decided that's where we'd go. The settlement check came, and she was serious. We left our husbands for good and took the leap ... me, my sister, her 3 kids, and 7 suitcases, on the greyhound bus, headed to South Carolina.

We both landed in Belton, South Carolina in 2003 and moved in with my youngest sister and her man until we were able to find a place. We had no idea what we were in for, but looking back I believe God sent us there to deliver our little sister out of bondage. This is my story so I won't tell all my sister's business except to say that she was in a very abusive relationship, and I thank God we came when we did, or I'm honestly not sure if she'd be alive today.

My big sister and I had gotten an apartment together in Belton, and in one of these episodes with our younger sister and her man, we persuaded her to leave him and come stay with us. He came to the apartment with a gun threatening to kill us all and we had to call the police. As a result we were evicted and ended up in Greenville living in what can only be described as a shack on the West side. This house had no interior doors, it was the craziest thing, and no heat or air. We used kerosene heaters in the winter, and fans in the summer.

We had nothing. We were sleeping on the floor, trying to find every resource to keep the lights on. The struggle was real. I remember that refrigerator being empty and getting food from Miracle Hill Food Bank on multiple occasions.

I finally got a job working at Resurgent Capital Services. We didn't have a car so my sister would walk me to work in the morning when it was still dark out, then meet me halfway coming back until we could afford bus fare. A job opening came up and she was able to get a job at the same place, so we ended up walking together to and from work. Grocery shopping was the worst, I just remember me, my sister and her kids would walk to the Walmart on Whitehorse Road from West Greenville, then carry all the groceries back. But we were eventually able to save up enough money to get a car and things were finally looking up. This was one of those places in my life where that old song makes the most sense to me: *"I've had some good days, I've had some hills to climb … I've had some weary days … and some lonely nights … but when I look around … and I think things over … All of my good days, outweigh my bad days … I won't complain."*

If we aren't careful, we can become so bitter about the journey that we aren't able to see how much we've grown along the way.

Wherever you are. Right Now. Give yourself credit for surviving the day before. Trust God for today. Seek God for tomorrow. And keep in mind the instructions and promise we have from The Father found in Philippians 4:6-7, "Be anxious for nothing, but in everything by prayer and supplication, with thanksgiving, let your requests be made known to God; and the peace of God, which surpasses all understanding, will guard your hearts and minds through Christ Jesus."

PURPOSE KNOCKS, TOO

One weekend a couple knocked on the door, asked if we had any prayer requests, gave us some banana bread and invited us to church. They were from Redemption World Outreach Center. At this time, I began attending Redemption under the leadership of Apostles Ron and Hope Carpenter. I had never experienced anything like this. So for me, their slogan at the time was fitting: *"Can't be explained, only experienced."*

First of all, I really never attended a truly multi-cultural ministry in my life. I was from a small, one-horse town in the Northwest, and I had never seen anything like this. Even when I lived in Oakland, the church we went to was completely African American, there wasn't a single person in that church of a different race.

I can truly say that I grew more spiritually at Redemption than at any time before in my life. After being raised in The Kingdom Hall which seemed to be all principle and no performance; then coming of age in the Pentecostal/Baptist churches, which seemed to be all performance and no principle, I found Apostle Carpenter's method of teaching so refreshing. The praise and worship experience was amazing. My thirst for God's word was revived and I truly began to heal and feel whole for the first time in a long time. If I had any complaint, it was that the "care pastors" assigned to me never reached out to me, not even once. At this time, the ministry was at least 5,000 members solid, and although there were small groups, hardly ever seeing the same face every Sunday and never really feeling connected took a toll on me after about 2 years. When I left there and went on to a smaller ministry to serve, I never heard from anyone, not a call or a note, nothing.

What I received during my time at Redemption is invaluable. The teaching I received from Apostle Carpenter renewed my faith in God, allowed me to heal, to breathe, and to recover from a long season in the wilderness. However, I will say this concerning any "mega-church" pastor, it is imperative that you remain in contact with your "Why". I've never pastored a church over 100 people let alone 5 or 10 thousand people, but what I do know, is you can't focus so much on the who, what, when, and where that you lose sight of the why. The Souls are the Why, the families are the Why, the communities are the Why. If you forget the Why, there will always be more members leaving out the back door than souls coming in the front.

It's impossible to successfully pastor an entire community of people whose pain and plight you have zero connection with beyond the pulpit. You may be able to get away with it for a while, especially if you have a very dedicated and anointed minister handling all your outreach in those at-risk communities. But after a series of incidents and dust-ups around sensitive topics concerning police brutality, NFL players kneeling, and other politically divisive events happening in our country, Apostle Ron decided to take a ministry opportunity in California and transfer the legacy he built in Greenville to Pastor John Gray, which has now become Relentless Church.

It's been a rough transition with no shortage of controversy, but it finally looks to be settling down. I am only mentioning that to say this, as a Pastor you are a pilot, and you are responsible for getting the passengers to a destination. Sometimes, you can be so focused on flying the plane that you forget who your passengers are. You have such a large network of "stewards and stewardesses" that you disconnect from the people, and by doing so you disconnect from what matters to them, their families, and their communities. I believe this is a lesson Apostle Carpenter has learned, and as I write this, he is preparing to bring his ministry back to Greenville, South Carolina with the launch of Redemption East. The entire process was fraught with missteps, mishaps, and misfires, but that is part of the process. As it concerns Redemption and Relentless, I wish them both the best. I pray that they flourish, and that as they go forward, their leaders will use the wisdom they've gained to build back better.

The "mega-church" experience I had is common to so many. It's a refreshing reprieve from the store-front, legalistic, segregated, buttoned-up, religious environments many of us came up in, but it's not perfect either. And sometimes, if you're not totally grounded in God, you can get caught up in the bells and whistles at first, but eventually get lost in a sea of faces, feeling like just another number in the building instead of a member of The Body. Being part of Redemption was something like a badge of honor, I was proud to associate myself with something so big. But I began to feel the pull of purpose in my spirit. I needed to be more than a number. I needed to do more than show up and receive, I had something to give to the Body as well.

I spent the next few years serving in various capacities at smaller ministries. Around the Summer of 2005, we moved to the Crossroads Apartments on Cleveland Street in Greenville. At this time, I was attending Greenville Technical College, still chasing that degree. I was walking home one day and managed to meet a young minister who was running an after-school program at the apartment complex. I became quick friends with him and his wife, Javion James, a remarkable Woman of God and Mompreneur who I still consider a sister and friend to this day.

I started working with the youth and he invited me to a revival at the ministry in the Southern Side area of Greenville he was attending at the time. The guest speaker of the night was Prophet Larry D. Reid … as he was referred to back then. These days he is the host of Larry Reid Live. I had been prophesied to before, but never with the level of specificity of Prophet Reid, you could say he read my mail. I stood there amazed as he told me things he had no way of knowing. He told me to stop wrapping up my sermons in poems and go ahead and preach the Gospel, that my poetry was a gift from God but I was using it as a crutch. He said, "I see notebooks and journals, everywhere in your house, notebooks everywhere in your house, keep writing, keep writing, keep writing, and write the book!" If you've ever heard him preach in person, he is very animated and can be just as loud, so he literally screamed this at me, rebuked me a bit, and basically told me to get my act together because the world was waiting for me to walk in my anointing. At just 24 years old, I was still trying to find myself, I didn't know if I was inspired or offended by this prophecy, but either way I knew he was telling the truth. And I believe, all these years later, the book is finally being written.

I ended up attending this church for a season and it was here that I began to really exercise my gift in ministry. The Pastor allowed me to hone the craft of spoken word and minister to the congregation on occasion. Eventually I was ordained as a Prophetess. I remember being so proud that day. Looking back, I realize it's impossible for another human being walking this earth in flesh to qualify your gift. The best he or she can do is affirm and equip you to do what God has already called you to do. Furthermore, if a man can give it to you, he can also take it away … or so he thinks.

It didn't take long for me to get past the honeymoon phase with this church. It became clear after about a year that the pastor was engaged in an extramarital affair with one of the members. It got so contentious that one day we were doing a community outreach event and the other woman dumped a pot of hotdog chili on the first lady. This was one of the sweetest women I've ever met, she would never make a scene. As for me, it took everything in me not to mollywop her ass on behalf of the First Lady. This wasn't the only incident, there were multiple small confrontations and dust-ups, but I brushed them aside believing I was in the right place because this is the first place my gift was acknowledged. When in reality, this was just another soul-tie. If you remember, I said in the last chapter that a soul-tie was a spiritual gateway to the soul accompanied by physical manifestations. So how can you have a soul-tie with a church?

I felt obligated to remain at this ministry because I was serving in leadership, I was working with the youth again and didn't want to leave them, but most importantly, this is the pastor that affirmed my call with an ordination, so I literally felt like I would be doing the pastor some kind of injustice, offending God in some way, or stepping out from under my "covering" if I left the church. So, I wasn't attending because God had instructed me, I was attending out of false obligation to a man and a ministry that was no longer edifying me in any way. But this situation had gotten too far out of hand and it was time to go.

I vowed that day that I was done attending this church. There was no way I was going to continue being part of the Jerry Springer Show, Church Edition. I finally got my nerve up and told the pastor I needed to talk to him. I don't remember everything I said, but I remember how he reacted. He almost cussed me out, accused me of trying to sabotage his ministry somehow, and told me to leave but I'm not licensed anymore and to bring "his ordination license" back and turn it in. That's exactly what I did too, brought his ordination license back, set it on the pulpit, walked out and never looked back. And see … that's what happens when you place the validity of your call into the hands of another human being.

I was heartbroken. I don't know what I expected but this wasn't it. I came home angry and crying from church that day. I ended up having a glass of wine, then another, and I actually got totally drunk that night and passed out. All of this behind a church! Now if that's not a soul-tie I don't know what is! I was literally grieving as if I'd just broken up with a boyfriend or fallen out with a close relative. So much of my spiritual identity and daily routine was wrapped up in my position in the church that it actually felt similar to a divorce. And like a divorce, the church and I had irreconcilable differences.

GOD. DID. NOT. CALL. ME. TO. DRAMA.

It's one thing to have an "incident" in the church, it's another thing for everyone to know what's going on and show up every Sunday, watch the First Lady play nice with the Side Chick, and for everybody to treat the pastor with honor and act like all of this is normal. Listen, anything you're doing that causes stress, anxiety, division, and confusion is not of God! The scriptures specifically speak on the matter in 1 Corinthians 14:33, "For God is not the author of confusion, but of peace, as in all churches of the saints."

You owe it to yourself, to be part of a ministry where the leadership is honoring their own call. If they aren't walking in the will of God themselves, how can they instruct you effectively? If they aren't authentic in their pursuit of God how can they direct traffic to the throne? Eventually, who and what they really are will be exposed. And if you aren't careful, you may find yourself drinking your sorrows away … or, getting angry with God and walking away from the church entirely.

I went from being a member of a church with over 5,000 members to serving in a church with less than 50 members, and both of them had issues. It's so easy to get caught up in the lights, camera, action of the mega-church environment. The production is usually flawless, praise and worship is like being at a concert Every Sunday, and it feels good to identify with a ministry that has such a recognizable presence in the community. But if you aren't independently grounded in God and his Word, it can quickly become just another club where you're simply an OnlyFan in a sea of thousands.

Storefront churches and large, traditional churches aren't any better. The people tend to be cliquish, territorial, and in some cases classist. And don't let it be a "family church" where one family makes up the majority of the membership, because they have a tendency to throw their weight around, the pastor is afraid to make any of them upset (that's if he's not related to them), and none of them can do any wrong. The bottom line is, no church is perfect, every church has issues, some are just better at hiding them. As I write this book, many spiritual leaders, great and small, are being exposed. It is imperative, now more than ever, that we have a relationship with God that is built on nothing less than our desire to seek him, serve him, and see him in others.

I can tell you that having membership in the thousands provides a great cover for failing leadership. Not everything growing is God, some of these ministries are swollen with infection, which makes it that much easier to mistake volume for virtue. On the other end, many of these smaller ministries are judged and mischaracterized as ineffective and unimportant, when some of the smaller churches are better equipped to reach the community directly and many of those pastors are preaching with more conviction and revelation than most mega-churches. It's so easy to be shallow when it comes to churches because we've all been programmed to believe that bigger is better. I don't know about you, but I'd rather be one of twenty people in a storefront building who are intentionally serving God and the community, than one of twenty thousand people showing up in an arena Sunday after Sunday to be entertained.

We are responsible for our own spiritual growth. And the moment we turn that responsibility over to the pulpit, we've already lost our way. Whether you're attending services in a 15,000 seat arena or a small church in the sticks, make sure you're sitting under leadership who hasn't lost sight of the Why, and no matter where you worship, make sure you never lose sight of the Who. If God is not being glorified. If you're not being edified. If there is any level of confusion or chaos. If you feel rejected, shunned, or singled out. If the leadership is failing in their personal walk with God. If you find yourself at any time, feeling more obligated than inspired to be present. It's time to go. You don't owe it to anyone or anything to sabotage your own spiritual well-being. Release yourself. Last Sunday was your last Sunday. Go with God and grow in grace.

All the versions of you that you didn't love,
brought you to the version of you,
that you are now.
Be grateful for every you—you've been.

LALAH DELIA

CHAPTER 3
ENTANGLEMENT

LET'S TALK ABOUT SEX

I loved her. I couldn't understand it, what was this? How did this happen? Twenty-Five years old, still trying to find myself, still lost, still broken. And she was a friend, a sister, a confidant. I don't even remember how it began, but here I am, on my back again, but this time it's different. I feel loved for the first time. I feel safe for the first time. I'm completely naked but I feel covered for the first time. This can't be right. This isn't right. So why does it feel so right? We were both in the church, and this went on for about 5 months. I love the Lord, I know who I am, I know what the Word of God says ... and, I loved her.

I've never been attracted to women this way, but I'm attracted to this one. Why? Maybe it was because she felt like clarity when nothing made sense. Maybe it was because she felt like a compass after being lost so long. Maybe it was because I felt safe enough to be weak in her presence. I never felt like I had to protect myself, my body, my heart from her. She was my best friend, and my lover. She seemed to be everything I needed. At some point I had to confront the fact that this was not who I was. But how do you just stop loving someone? I realized it wasn't about her at all, this was another manifestation of My Brokenness. I decided it was over, I told her I enjoyed spending time with her, but I've always preferred men, that I was called to preach, and this is not who I am. Sounds crazy doesn't it? But that's exactly what I said. She agreed that it was not who she was either. We were both believers, caught up, and entangled. But, confessing the truth is not enough to live it. I decided to empty myself and purge my soul with prayer. I fasted for five days ... no food, no water. I don't know if I ever felt that tormented in my life, but I came out of that fast "delivered" ... if that's a thing. I didn't tell a soul about it. It was over.

I want to pause here to take an opportunity to say that I do not believe in conversion therapy. I do not believe in guilting, condemning, and beating people into behavioral modification and spiritual submission. I do not believe it is effective and I do not believe God would want that for anyone. This is my journey, my experience, and my testimony. The reason I believe this was a season in my life and not a place I could continue to exist, is because it is not who I am at my core. But for some, this is not and never was a choice they made, it has always been who they are.

Some may say, how can you say that and call yourself a Christian? I'm too real to be fake! So many Christians have had similar experiences but are too ashamed to testify about it for fear of being judged and shunned by the church. Even I wondered whether I should include this part of my testimony, but concerning the topic of "church hurt" how could I possibly leave it out? Many are in undercover relationships in the church, from the pulpit to the pews. Some are in flat-out denial about their sexuality altogether. In my personal opinion, everyone has the propensity for duality in sexual preference depending on any given set of variables from childhood trauma, to relationship trauma, to self-control or lack thereof, up to and including, which is likely the most controversial reason, biological and/or genetic makeup. And if you weren't clear what I meant by that last part, yes, I am saying that some people are simply born that way. We do not get to say that they are not Children of God or exclude them from grace just because they are wired differently.

And to answer the question, how do you just stop loving someone? You don't. She is still close to my heart. My relationship with her is still, to this day, the only relationship I've been in that ended leaving no residue of resentment, bitterness, or brokenness to heal from. I literally parted ways with my best friend in pursuit of my purpose. She accepted that and moved on without making me her enemy, which in my personal experience, is something men have a terrible time doing. When things don't work out, all of a sudden you become a bitch or a hoe, but you weren't all that while you were sleeping together. We handled it maturely, without drama, like grown women, and to this day there is nothing but respect between us. And while I can be honest enough to admit that I enjoyed her physically, even after all the pain I've endured at the hands of men, there is still nothing like being held and loved by a man who knows how to handle himself with a woman sexually.

Sex has become so taboo in the church, to the point the church has made it something dirty, and don't be gay because then you're really busting hell wide open. When the truth of the matter is, this flesh just wants to be satisfied, and aside from our personal preferences, the flesh does not care how it is fulfilled. I choose to be with men, because that is what I am predominantly attracted to, but so many do not feel like they have that choice.

I know I'm not going to make many friends with this, and may even lose some, but many will be surprised to know that God loves gays and lesbians. Why? Because God loves everyone! Furthermore, it is my personal opinion that you can be a believer who identifies as Christian *and* be a member of the LGBTQ+ community.

Did you know the English word "homosexual" did not exist in *any* Bible until 1946? It was added to the Revised Standard Version, which was a translation compiled and published by a team of 22 men at Yale University under the leadership of Luther Allan Weigle. It was a seminary student who challenged their use of the word "homosexual" as a translation of the Greek words *malakoi* and *arsenokoitai* in 1 Corinthians 6:9, backed up by an exhaustive outline of his research and reasoning. In response to this, Weigle and the RSV committee decided the word "homosexual" was an inaccurate translation and replaced it with "sexual perverts".

So how did it end up in our present-day versions of the Bible? Even though the RSV Committee agreed the translation was a misinterpretation, Weigle had signed a contract stating that he would not make any revisions to the RSV for 10 years. In the span of those 10 years, other translation teams were working on various versions of the Bible. These versions used the RSV as their basis for including the word "homosexual" in their translations, without knowing the RSV Committee had retracted its decision.[2] This may be a perfect example of the scripture in Galatians 5:9 "a little leaven, leavens the whole lump." And now, after 75 years of this error being perpetuated

---

2   https://baptistnews.com/article/my-quest-to-find-the-word-homosexual-in-the-bible/#.YovvNS-B1B1

in seminaries and sanctuaries, we have an entire generation of pastors committed to preaching a scripture out of context in order to convince entire congregations that homosexuality itself is a sin and to condemn gay people to hell.

As far as I'm concerned there aren't any more gay people going to hell (if you believe it even exists) than anyone else. What is the foundation for this reasoning? Well let's see what the Bible has to say. First, let's start with 1 Corinthians 6:9-10 (the same being similarly repeated in 1 Timothy 1:9-10) since this is where most Christians begin and end the conversation. I want to give 5 interpretations of this scripture (as I understand it after thorough research), so at least you are clear about the foundation for my position even if you don't agree:

- **Original Greek Script (53-54 CE):** [9]"Η οὐκ οἴδατε ὅτι ἄδικοι θεοῦ βασιλείαν [1] οὐ κληρονομήσουσιν; μὴ πλανᾶσθε οὔτε πόρνοι οὔτε εἰδωλολάτραι οὔτε μοιχοὶ οὔτε *μαλακοὶ οὔτε ἀρσενοκοῖται* [10]οὔτε κλέπται οὔτε πλεονέκται, οὐ μέθυσοι, οὐ λοίδοροι, οὐχ ἅρπαγες βασιλείαν θεοῦ κληρονομήσουσιν.

- **Geneva Bible (1599):** [9]Know ye not that the unrighteous shall not inherit the kingdom of God? [a]Be not deceived: neither fornicators, nor idolaters, nor adulterers, *nor wantons, nor buggerers*, [10]Nor thieves, nor covetous, nor drunkards, nor railers, nor extortioners shall inherit the kingdom of God.

- **King James Version (1611):** [9]Know ye not that the unrighteous shall not inherit the kingdom of God? Be not deceived: neither fornicators, nor idolaters, nor adulterers,

59

nor effeminate, nor abusers of themselves with mankind, [10]Nor thieves, nor covetous, nor drunkards, nor revilers, nor extortioners, shall inherit the kingdom of God.

- **New Revised Standard (1989):** [9]Do you not know that wrongdoers will not inherit the kingdom of God? Do not be deceived! Fornicators, idolaters, adulterers, *male prostitutes, sodomites,* [10]thieves, the greedy, drunkards, revilers, robbers—none of these will inherit the kingdom of God.

- **The Message Bible (1993):** [9-10]Don't you realize that this is not the way to live? Unjust people who don't care about God will not be joining in his kingdom. *Those who use and abuse each other, use and abuse sex, use and abuse the earth and everything in it,* don't qualify as citizens in God's kingdom.

Now I'm sure you're wondering why I gave so many translations of this scripture (and be honest, you probably didn't read them). The point is I want you to see how much the interpretation of this Scripture changed from one culture to the next, from one translation to the next, from one century to the next, and how we have allowed our very narrow interpretation of God's Word to create a false, judgmental perspective about an entire community of people, which is totally antithetical to the Word of God.

You may be wondering why I'm spending so much time on this topic, the reason is the LGBTQ+ community has been historically rejected, ostracized, judged, and abused by the church on a level that far exceeds any other marginalized group in my opinion. And where they should be able to go to find love, God, healing, and acceptance is the very place that has closed their minds, hearts, and doors to them. Even if you're not part of this community, don't skip over this chapter, because everyone knows at least one person who is gay and even if you don't, all of us could use a greater understanding, empathy, and open heart toward our brothers and sisters in Christ ... yes, In Christ.

Notice I started with the Greek text, and the reason for that is because Christians generally begin with the King James Bible (KJV) and go from there, but what we need to understand is the King James Bible is not the original text, it is the text as translated by the scholars commissioned by King James I of England in 1611, and also as understood and influenced by their collective ideologies and culture of that era. Not only is it not the original text, it is not even the first translation of the text. There were 11 English translations of the Bible before the King James Version, dating all the way back to 1380, which is why I included The Geneva Bible, one of the most prominent translations that predate the King James Version by 51 years. Knowing this is critical to understanding the posture of the Church toward the LGBTQ+ community.

So, let's take a moment and break this down. The Greek version of the text I want to focus on is "μαλακοὶ οὔτε ἀρσενοκοῖται" ... well what the heck is that?! The first word is Malakos, which is an adjective that literally means "squishy" but is understood in context to be defined as soft or effeminate. The second word is Arsenokoitēs, which is so rare in ancient Greek it is said that there is no other record of its use predating the Bible. This word is a blend of the word "arsen" which is one of the Greek words for male, and "koite", the Greek word for bed, which when put together roughly translates to "malebedders" or more commonly sodomites. It is these two words that have shaped the church's present-day interpretation of the term "homosexuality", so let's dissect this a bit.

If you notice each one of these translations interprets these words differently. Unlike arsenokoitēs, the first word, malakos, is found in other writings of the time, and is more commonly used as an indictment of cowardice and sometimes vanity, or other characteristics thought to be feminine in nature. The sexual connotation of this word is usually referred to as "kinaidia" not malakos. One could argue that it doesn't even refer to sexual orientation or sexual acts at all, but it is likely a sexual reference given the context of the scripture in that it is listed just after "μοιχοὶ" ("moichos" in Greek, which is adultery) and right before Arsenokoitēs ("malebedders" or men who take active roles in non-procreative sex). This word has been translated and understood to mean everything from prostitution to nymphomania (wantons; lacking self-control). A more realistic interpretation would be that this applies to those using their bodies for profit and those being reckless with their bodies by casually engaging in sexual acts without consideration of risk, regardless of whether it is with males or females.

Now on to arsenokoitēs, which I believe is the most complicated to explain and therefore understand. Let me remind you that this word is rare, it has not been found to have a contemporary use outside of the Bible, and its translation has varied throughout the centuries depending on the interpretations, language, culture, and ideologies of the translators.

The Greek word Arsenokoitēs is translated to "masculorum concubitoribus" in the Vulgata Clementina, a 1592 medieval Latin translation of the Bible by Pope Clement VIII, which implies pimping. The 1602 Reina-Valera Spanish translation of the Bible by Casiodoro de Reina, uses the phrase "los sodomitas" (the sodomites). French theologian David Martin's La Bible of 1744 translates the passage to "ceux qui commettent des péchés contre nature" (those who commit sins against nature). The same word is translated to "Knabenschänder" in Martin Luther's 1545 German translation, and "quelli che usano co' maschi" in the Italian translation found in the 1649 Giovanni Deodati Bible, both of which translate in English to the sexual abuse of children or pedophilia.

I could give more translations, but the point is none of them used the term "homosexual" when translating this scripture. I think it's safe to say none of them approved of same-sex relationships either. However, given the wide variation in translation, the historically uncommon and rarely used Greek word "arsenokoitēs" seems to cover anything thought to be sexually unnatural or immoral including pimping, prostitution, pedophilia, rape, bestiality and sodomy, none of which are exclusive to the LGBTQ+ community.

Since this word means different things, to different people, in different languages, and different cultures, over the course of many centuries, it is my personal opinion that the Message Bible gives the most accurate present-day interpretation, which simply states "Those who use and abuse each other, use and abuse sex, use and abuse the earth and everything in it, don't qualify as citizens in God's kingdom." It doesn't get any plainer than that! This translation captures the intent of the writer, which is to say that using sex in any way that endangers yourself, others, or God's creation is immoral.

Ascribing this behavior to one community is shallow, short-sighted, and also immoral. The absence of character, self-control, and moral deprivation that causes one to engage in reckless sexual behavior is not exclusive to the LGBTQ+ community. Sexual abuse and the propensity to use sex as a weapon is about power and control over the victim, not sexual orientation. Nearly 99% of sexual predators are men, and most of them identify as heterosexual, even those who sexually abuse members of the same sex.

Now that we've got a clear understanding of what the scripture actually says and intended vs. what has been traditionally taught in church, let's deal with the fact that no matter how you interpret these words, they are part of a list. They aren't singled out, separated, or printed in All Caps. They are part of a list of actions and practices that serve to disinherit us from the Kingdom of God. A list that includes idol worship, adultery, greed, theft, alcoholism, abusers, conmen, scammers, and "those who do wrong" in general. In addition to these things, the Bible explicitly names 7 things God hates and considers an abomination in Proverbs 6:16-19, which are "haughty eyes, a lying tongue, hands that shed innocent blood, a heart that devises wicked schemes, feet that are quick to rush into evil, a false witness who pours out lies, and a person who stirs up conflict in the community." Galatians 5:19-21 adds to the list uncleanness, witchcraft, hostility, hatred, quarreling, jealousy, fits of rage, selfish ambition, division (disunity, not math), and revelries (rambunctious partying) to name a few, and again ends by informing us that anyone engaging in these things "will not inherit the Kingdom of God."

I don't know about you, but I've seen all of these things right up in the church! Every single one of them! And if we're honest, all of us have engaged in one or more of these over the course of our lifetime and still struggle with some of them (have you gotten angry and engaged in any arguments lately?). So, if gays are going to hell so are the deacons smoking cigarettes behind the church. So is the man beating his wife or the mother abusing her children. So is the drug addict and the alcoholic. So is the greedy businessman and the shady salesman. So is the pastor cheating on his wife with the church secretary. So is the college freshman partying at the frat house. So is the hoarder who, for mental or other reasons, keeps an unclean, filthy home. So is everyone who goes back through the buffet line after they're already full. So is the one causing division in the church or the community. So are people who can't control their temper. So are racists, xenophobes, homophobes, and bigots. I could go on, but the bottom line is no one is going to hell for being gay!

How can I be so certain? Because I take God at his Word. John 3:16 says, "For God so loved the world that he gave his only begotten Son, that whoever believes in him should not perish but have everlasting life." Notice that the scripture doesn't say "However" but "Whoever"? In the church we have modified this scripture with our actions to add however, if you love like me … however, if you look like me … however, if you believe like me … and as of late, however, if you vote like me … you shall not perish but have everlasting life. But God has placed no such restrictions on our access to salvation.

God instructs us to abide in his love, and more specifically in John 15:12 says, "This is My commandment, that you love one another as I have loved you." Therefore, the mandate of the church and so-called Christian is to love God and love people … not people you like, people who look like you, dress like you, go to your church, sing in your choir, make the money you make, go to the college you went to, believe in the God you believe in, belong to your political party, or love like you love … no, all people. This was a stretch for those who literally walked with Christ, it's no wonder the concept is nearly impossible for many Christians to grasp. But for those of us who walk with Christ more than we ride with religion, there is too much evidence in the Word of God to ignore the Will of God … which is the Heart of God concerning how we treat those who don't fit neatly within the confines of our comfort zone. The Apostle Peter put it perfectly in Acts 10:28 when he was called by God to minister to the house of Cornelius, a centurion in what was known as the Italian Regiment.

> Then he said to them, "You know how unlawful it is for a Jewish man to keep company with or go to one of another nation. *But God has shown me* that I should not call any man common or unclean. (emphasis mine)

As human beings we naturally have certain built-in prejudices, all of us do. Whether by virtue of environment or by example. But if we say we believe in God, and further say we believe in God's Word, we simply cannot read his Word without application ... daily, practical application. We can't ignore God's intent and instruction to "love they neighbor as thyself" when God has gone out of his way to show us, just as he showed the Apostle Peter.

The truth is complicated and uncomfortable, but it is the truth nevertheless. Understand that I agree with everything God says in his Word (not historical texts added to the Word, translations, and misinterpretations of men). I am certainly not sugar-coating anything, but the greater example is how Christ conducted himself on the earth. Not one time did Christ condemn anyone to hell. The closest he came to it was his rebuke of the church. So I refuse to send people to hell or make a declaration that they are going to hell and I find the audacity of anyone who thinks they have the authority to do so comical at least and reckless at most.

Let me give you a scenario to consider, a while back there was a young lady by the name of Mokgadi Caster Semenya who made the news because she was an Olympic track star who, after competing very well, was banned because it was "discovered" she had "undescended testicles" and no womb after hormone testing. In other words, she had the plumbing of a female on the outside, but she was internally male. The condition has many names but the one I will use is Intersex. There are also many cases where children are born with both organs and the parents choose one for them, then they later grow up to be the opposite. Let me ask you a question, if she is attracted to women does that make her a lesbian? And if so, why? Because she has a vagina does that automatically make her female? Because a man has a penis does that automatically make him male? Or is it deeper than that?

Sexual orientation and gender are not mere physical matters, they are a compilation of biological, neurological, and psychological factors. There are many who have had a course change because of trauma, abuse, or other external factors, and they most certainly can be delivered because they were never that way in the first place. Then there are others who, regardless of what they look like on the outside, are hard-wired exactly opposite. How can Semenya, how can other people like her be "Delivered" from who they are?

Who would make a conscious decision to exist between worlds—not here and not there—undefined yet labeled by society's norms? Are you saying God, in his infinite wisdom, does not understand they psychological, hormonal, biological, neurological, and any number of reasons why a man may be attracted to men, or why a woman may be attracted to women? Are you saying that Semenya and others like her should not be able to love someone and be loved by someone because they cannot physically fit into the strictly defined mold of a man or woman?

Now listen, seeing two guys kiss may make you throw up in your mouth a little bit, but you do not know all the factors surrounding a same-sex attraction. And while it may be biologically unnatural—as in it does not reproduce life—to throw a religious blanket on everything and say they all need to repent or go to hell is not only inconsistent with scripture but inconsiderate, uncompassionate, ignorant, and ultimately damaging to the mission of the church.

I am a minister, not a theologian, but I understand the Word of God very well. I know and believe we have been called to be salt and light in the Earth, not to poor salt in wounds, and blind people with light. I actually believe if Jesus were walking the earth today many Christians would be trying to send him to hell for some of the radical things he would be doing and some of the people he would call friends. I want to challenge you to educate yourself about the many medical complexities of sexual orientation and attraction. You will find that it is not nearly as simple as men should be attracted to women, women should be attracted to men, and if not you need to be delivered, repent, and get right or go to hell. God has called us to a level of compassion that we cannot even maintain unless we strive at it daily with help from the Holy Spirit.

Thank God no one in the flesh gets to determine who does and doesn't go to hell, because if we did, I'm 100% certain we'd all go. You cannot live right enough to earn your way to heaven. Jesus is our Righteousness; his Blood is our admission fee and it is paid in full! Therefore, Christians would do well to repent from the sin of self-righteousness, and learn the art of compassion, which Jesus so passionately and flawlessly exemplified. Let's take away the L, G, B, T, Q and what you have are people, created by God, breathing his breath, with his Spirit inside of them, just like everyone else.

I read an article about a transgender teen named Josh Alcorn, who was born male but identified as female and it broke my heart. Leelah, as she preferred to be called, said she felt like a girl trapped in a boy's body since she was 4 years old. And at the age of 14 she was killed in an apparent act of suicide after being struck by a tractor-trailer on Interstate 71 in Kings Mills, Ohio. In a suicide note posted to Tumblr, which she programmed to publish after her death, she wrote "After 10 years of confusion I finally understood who I was. I immediately told my mom, and she reacted extremely negatively, telling me that it was a phase, that I would never truly be a girl, that God doesn't make mistakes, that I am wrong. If you are reading this, parents, please don't tell this to your kids. Even if you are Christian or are against transgender people don't ever say that to someone, especially your kid. That won't do anything but make them hate them self. That's exactly what it did to me."

She talks about how she battled depression and goes on to say "My mom started taking me to a therapist, but would only take me to Christian therapists, (who were all very biased) so I never actually got the therapy I needed to cure me of my depression. I only got more Christians telling me that I was selfish and wrong and that I should look to God for help." Sadly, the very place she should've been able to come to for guidance, love, acceptance, and understanding helped to push her over the edge into hopelessness. My thoughts are, Leelah would rather leave this world than live in a world, more specifically a family, that refused to accept that how she's wired on the inside doesn't match how she's built on the outside and there's no amount of repenting, counseling, or behavior modification that would change that.

Leelah is one of thousands of LGBTQ youth who committed suicide that year. A 2011 study by the National Center for Transgender Equality found that 41% of 6,450 responding transgender and gender nonconforming people had attempted suicide. In 2018 JAMA

Pediatrics compiled data from 35 previous studies. The analysis involved close to 2.4 million heterosexual youth and 113,468 LGBTQ youth, ages 12 to 20, from 10 countries. The results included the following LGBT suicide statistics:

- LGBTQ youth were 3.5 times as likely to attempt suicide as their heterosexual peer.

- Transgender teens were 5.87 times more likely.

- Gay and lesbian youth were 3.71 times more likely.

- Bisexual youth were 3.69 times more likely to attempt suicide than teens who identified as heterosexual.

Furthermore, the national Youth Risk Behavior Survey (YRBS), conducted by the Centers for Disease Control and Prevention, found that 40 percent of high school students who identify as gay, lesbian, or bisexual or questioning (unsure of their orientation) have seriously considered suicide.

At just 16 years old, Leelah said she realized her "parents would never come around" … in other words, they would never accept her for who she was, she could never live up to their expectations, and they would never love her like Christ loves her—and everyone else like her—unconditionally. Listen, if you're reading this book right now and you identify as lesbian, gay, bisexual, transgender, or queer I want you to know God loves you, God made you, he knows what you are, he understands even if no one else does, and you are *not* a mistake! The fact that you exist is not a sin!

I promise you, no matter what your parents say, your family says, your church says, or society says, your life matters, you have purpose, Jesus loves you, and he wants you to live! If you need to speak with someone or are currently in a crisis, please visit www.thetrevorproject. org for resources in your area, text 678-678, or call (866) 488-7386 to speak with counselors 24/7/365.

My question to the church is, are we really going to continue to remain ignorant about the complicated nature of gender identity? Are we really going to continue rejecting children of God simply because they love differently? Are we really going to continue damning an entire population of human beings to hell by applying the law to them, but grace to ourselves? Are we really going to continue being the hypocrites and vipers Jesus spoke of in Matthew 23:33? And if so, how can we continue to call ourselves Christian? As Jesus said, how will we escape hell?

I have friends and family who are gay, and guess what, I believe wholeheartedly that I will see them in the Kingdom of Heaven! Why? Because I also know these people believe Jesus is their Lord and Savior … funny how that's the only prerequisite given in John 3:16 before "…shall have everlasting life." Now, let me make this clear for all the "Super-Religious, Holier Than Thou, My Sin is Better Than Yours" saints … I'm not saying you can "live any kinda way" and call yourself a Christian. What I'm saying is, salvation is not a social club for perfect people! It's actually a privilege extended to us by God through grace for imperfect people. If you have a bad attitude, break the speed limit, don't wear your seatbelt, think thoughts that are contrary to the Word of God (even if you don't act on them), and I could go on … What makes you think you're going to Heaven, but gay people are going to Hell, when you both believe Jesus is the Messiah?

I really wish the saints would stop ostracizing and singling out Gay People as the Red-Headed Stepchildren (no offense to people with red hair) of the Church! (unless they can sing or play the keyboard

71

really well, then it's ok to put them in the Music Ministry and give them a salary—hypocrites!). There are gay people in committed relationships that these fake—sitting in church—not sleeping in the same bed—haven't talked since the last argument—sleeping around in the church—hating each other but too religious to get divorced—heterosexual married couples can't hold a candle to! But somehow you believe God honors your raggedy-ass excuse for a marriage?

And since I'm here, let me drop some hot sauce on this thing, if you practice anal sex with your wife it's still sodomy. It's not any more natural for a man to sodomize a woman than it is for a man to sodomize a man ... but the marriage bed is undefiled isn't that what they preach? I've got news for you, our genitalia are distinct, but our asses are all the same. You know what else is unnatural, as in a sexual act that does not produce life? Oral sex. Yep, how's that for keeping it real for all my Kinky McFreaky Saints. But hey, if that's your thing, It's your bed, and it's your business! Who doesn't want to swing from the chandelier occasionally? But I'm certain neither anal nor oral sex is what God had in mind when he commanded Adam to be fruitful and fill the Earth. Yet, many in the church enjoy them. And guess what, that's ok, do your thing! Just don't think you're any better than anyone else doing their thing, because you are not.

I am not perfect. Because I'm not perfect, I don't have time to send people to hell because of their imperfections! And if you really, really, really believe what Jesus The Christ did on the cross actually worked ... I want to challenge you right now, to keep your judgment to yourself, stay in your lane, mind the business in your own bedroom, and exemplify Jesus Christ by doing the best you can every day to Love God and Love People.

If we can manage to do this, maybe the next time someone in the LGBTQ+ community walks into the church, they may find Christ there and decide life is worth living, because just like everybody else, God loves them. Not the version of them we're comfortable with. God loves them right now, even as they are. Instead of being further traumatized by fake church folks, Sadducees, and Pharisees, sitting high looking low, acting like they've got the monopoly on grace, when they can't even understand the miracle, mass, and gravity of salvation, because they've accepted Jesus, but rejected Christ.

WAP

Dark chocolate. Infectious laugh. Brilliant mind. Unwavering ambition. I was addicted before I even took a hit. He showed up on my porch one day, accompanied by a mutual friend. He had this million-dollar business venture and my friend thought he could use my help. In her words, "I know somebody who can straighten you out." They sat in my living room and pitched the business to me and my mother. The whole time arguing, debating ... and for some reason, she felt the need to keep mentioning that he was an ex-felon. Apparently, this had been a roadblock that kept the project from being financed. I heard her, but I was intrigued, I wanted to know more ... about him.

I began working with him on the project and it wasn't long before it became more than business. The chemistry between us was thicker than molasses. I was falling ... hard. He was intelligent, sexy, and saved. What's not to love?! I remember he used to call me Honeycomb. I asked him why and he told me I reminded him of the scriptures (Psalm 119:104) because I was sweeter than honey. He had game for days. It would be a long time before I realized I was being played.

I met him in June 2011. By this time, I had founded The Restoration Center and was pastoring a small, but growing congregation out of The Coffee Underground in downtown Greenville. I also started a non-profit homeless ministry called U-Turn Outreach Ministries. We had 6 transitional houses in partnership with the Upstate Homeless Coalition. I was focused, the ministry was doing well, and I felt like I was finally walking in my purpose. I had no idea that the day he showed up at my house would be the beginning of the end of everything I had struggled so hard to build.

I began spending more and more time at the office, writing grants, hosting investor meetings, attending networking events, and working late nights. My focus on the ministry was slowly slipping. During one of our late-night brainstorming sessions I found out he was living in the office. When I asked him what was going on, he said he had to choose between maintaining an apartment or maintaining the business and he chose the business. I admired that. I was actually inspired by it. At this time, I was single, no kids, living in a 3-bedroom home near downtown Greenville, it was just me and my mom. I asked if he wanted to stay with me until he could get everything up and going. I don't have to tell you this was big mistake ... and this is not a romance novel so I'm not going to bore you with the details of how it happened ... but you can catch it in the movie (speaking that into existence).

If you haven't been under a rock, in a cave, somewhere beneath sea-level, then you know that "WAP" was one of the most popular songs to hit the airwaves in 2020. All these preachers came out speaking against Cardi B and Megan and how they weren't good role models for young girls. The whole narrative irritated me. First of all, Cardi B and Megan never said they were role models for young girls. And who are these Christian parents entrusting the well-being of their daughters to the hip hop industry? Ultimately parents are responsible for what their children consume, so to berate the world, for being the world, and creating material for the world, is a wasted exercise. Furthermore, as many "certified freaks" as there are in the church, I found it to be hypocritical. Most of the things they're talking about in that song many Christians enjoy, so they can do it in their bedrooms, but to put it in song and verse is a cardinal sin? Miss me. If you listen to Amazing Grace while you get it on then do your thing, as for me … let me tell you how I got this ring.

"WAP" samples the 1990s Baltimore club classic, "Whores In This House" by Frank Ski. Let's talk about the whore in "this house" and your house. Everybody has done something they're not proud of and wouldn't want anybody to know. I've been the wife … and the side chick … I've been the enabler and the addict … I've been hurt and I've hurt people. One of the biggest issues I have with "church folk" is the façade of perfection. Especially in the pulpit.

The bottom line is every single one of us are engaged in a lifelong War Against Purpose. Each one of us has slipped, tripped, and stumbled trying to walk this narrow road. Each one of us has said things we wish we could take back … made decisions we wish we could back track. I am no exception.

Remember I told you the doctor said I may not be able to have children and would likely need fertility treatment in order to get pregnant? Lies. There I was, pregnant with my first child at 31 years old … with my live-in boyfriend … out of wedlock. Did I tell you I was pastoring a church? Hot mess. How did this happen?! I mean … besides the birds and bees edition. Pride. Pride is how it happened. We always think we can handle it; we always think we're stronger in the Lord than we really are.

And it don't take much to get slapped with the reminder that these hoes ain't loyal! Yes, the "whores in the house" that everybody battles with. Everybody has thorns ... thoughts, desires, and the propensity to sin that exists in every human being. These things don't disappear because we get "saved" or wash off in the baptism pool.

And here's what the church won't tell you: God never intended for us to be sin-free. Say what? Yes, let me say it again for the folks in the back. God never intended for us to be sin-free. It has always been his desire for us to be free from sin. Which also leaves us with the option and opportunity to be free to sin. It's called free will, and all of us have it.

If you believe in the story of creation, then you know about the Tree of the Knowledge of Good and Evil, which God instructed them not to eat of, but did not make it inaccessible to them. In other words, from the foundation of the earth, God has always wanted us to choose him, then turned around and sent his son anyway knowing that we wouldn't always ... couldn't always do so. There is a constant battle between what we know to do and what we want to do. The Apostle Paul put it this way in Romans 7:21-25, "I have discovered this principle of life—that when I want to do what is right, I inevitably do what is wrong. I love God's law with all my heart. But there is another power within me that is at war with my mind. This power makes me a slave to the sin that is still within me," he goes on to say "Oh, what a miserable person I am! Who will free me from this life that is dominated by sin and death? Thank God! The answer is in Jesus Christ our Lord. So, you see how it is: In my mind I really want to obey God's law, but because of my sinful nature I am a slave to sin." This is me. This is you. This is us.

The term "entanglement" became a popular catch phrase and the source of endless memes of Will Smith after Jada used the term to explain her encounter with August Alsina during a Red Table episode. Everybody had something to say about it, cracking jokes, and making light of what is actually a very serious situation for a married couple to endure and survive. Folks were basically making a big deal of her use of the word "entanglement" vs. cheating or adultery, but this was probably the most accurate description of what happened.

It was more than an affair; it was more than cheating. If you listened closely to what she was saying, it wasn't even about August Alsina as much as it was about years of unaddressed issues and a lack of honesty with herself and her husband. It was unfulfilled physical, emotional, and spiritual needs. It was an entanglement. Here's the thing, we only know about it because they're celebrities. But how many of us have been entangled right up in the church? It's so easy to be judgmental when our own skeletons are safe in the closet. Bottom line is "all have sinned and fallen short of the glory" (Romans 3:23), but for some reason this fact is too often drowned out by judgment in the church, and usually by folks who have simply perfected their public presentations.

It's me. I'm folks. I used to be anyway. But there's nothing like good old-fashioned humility to cure a judgmental spirit. There I was, pastoring and pregnant. Preaching and pregnant. Praying and pregnant. And to top it off, I found out he was cheating on me.

It was another busy day at the office, investors coming and going, and his phone was about to die. He was expecting a very important call, so he hands me the phone and asks me to go charge it or find his charger. Something explicit popped up on the phone, so of course I had to see what this was about. And there it is. An entire relationship with another woman; his son's mother.

I was so mad I was ready to turn everything over, but I had to maintain my decorum with investors present in the office. It also happened that this day I was also scheduled for one of my first prenatal appointments.

I handed him back the phone and left the office. He knew something was up, but he was tied up and couldn't make a scene.

So, I was sitting in the parking lot of Greenville Memorial Hospital, crying and angry. I was so angry at myself for getting myself into this mess. At this time no one knew I was pregnant except my mother ... she dreamed about fish one night and wasted no time interrogating me first thing the following morning. For those who are unfamiliar, in African American culture, when a family's matriarch dreams of fish it is widely believed to be a sign that someone in the family is pregnant ... in this instance, it was apparently my turn. And for a brief moment, a millisecond, the thought of abortion came across my mind. I immediately dismissed the idea. But let me tell you why I'm confessing this. The thought of public embarrassment and a lifelong connection to a man I wasn't even sure loved me was enough to make me at least think about it. It wasn't enough to make me go through with it, or even entertain it, but it was an option that presented itself never-the-less.

There's a reason why the adversary presented this to me -and yes, I believe it was the Adversary. We all have a reflex called self-preservation. It's not something you have to learn or be trained to do, it's not even something you have to practice. If you trip and fall right now, you will naturally grasp for stability and position yourself as you are falling to alleviate the consequences of tripping. We even preserve things we care about or love by reflex. Have you ever stopped hard on the brakes and had a loved one in the passenger seat? If you cared anything about them, you extended your arm in front of them, even if they had a seatbelt on. Why? Self-Preservation.

When it came to my life, reputation, and the consequences of having this man's baby, I had the option of preserving myself over preserving this life. All I had to risk was my reputation and the thought crossed my mind. I cannot even imagine what it must be like for a young woman who is raped and must consider incubating the life of her rapist and then seeing him in the face of her own child. I can't imagine being faced with the probability of my child being born with a debilitating disability or terminal illness. I can't imagine being told I will not be able to come to term safely and to do so would be to risk both my life and that of my unborn child, then having to choose whether to commit homicide or risk committing a double suicide. I can't imagine being a 17 year old high school student with my whole life in front me trying to decide if I'm ready to be a mother or if I want to hang on to my dreams, keep my scholarship, and go on to college (which is never a decision the father of the child is burdened with). How trivial does a reputation sound in light of all this? And yet, I thought about it.

The church has a bad habit of trying to ramrod Jesus into people's bedrooms, classrooms, uteruses, and voting booths. They do this with zero example from Christ or instruction in the Scripture to do so. I did not decide to have an abortion, but I don't judge anyone who does. Why? Because I understand. Even if I can't personally relate, I understand that it's not my business what other people do with their bodies.

This may sound like a contradiction, but I am Anti-Abortion and Pro-Choice. How can I be both? It's simple. I believe that if at all possible and whenever safe for the mother, a baby should be allowed to come to term and live, even if the mother decides to put the child up for adoption. However, I understand that there may be reasons why a mother either doesn't believe this is an option or doesn't accept it as an option. But whatever the reasoning is, it's her body and her choice. One that she should be allowed to make in consultation with her doctor and loved ones if necessary. I also do not believe God intended for Christians to use government systems to enforce Scripture.

The church is ridiculously hypocritical when it comes to this. We want to shout "Separation of Church and State" when it's convenient, but when we want to regulate who people marry or whether they should have children, then we want the Church to be the state. There is no example of Jesus engaging in politics to force unbelievers to accept him as Savior or yield to the commandments of God. Yet, that is what so many Christians are doing, and it has gotten so bad that there have been self-proclaimed Christians picketing, intimidating and screaming at Planned Parenthood staff and clients, threatening to bomb abortion clinics or trying to assassinate doctors in the name of "saving babies".

We have to step back and ask ourselves, is this what Jesus would do? If Jesus were walking the earth today, would he be outside on the picket line with the religious fanatics drenched in fake blood screaming baby killers at the top of his lungs? Or would he be sitting beside the 15-year-old rape victim in the waiting room, holding her hand, not speaking, not judging, simply reassuring her with his presence alone that neither life, nor death, can separate her from his love?

The Bible says, "choose this day whom you will serve" (Joshua 24:15) yet, Christians seek to take that choice away from people. They want to choose who you can marry, they want to choose when and how you have children, they want to choose who you vote for, they even want to choose how you address matters important to you. Many of these same Christians who are shouting "Pro-Life" from the rooftops were silent while the world watched a police officer kneel on the neck of George Floyd for 8 minutes and 46 seconds. They are silent while children are being snatched from their parents and orphanized by the United States Government. They are silent while immigrant women are being given forced hysterectomies. They are silent while black and brown bodies are being gunned down in the streets. It amazes me how zealous Christians are about unborn babies, but how unbothered they are about dead bodies ... especially black and brown bodies. This situation falls perfectly into the list of "woes" given in Matthew 23:23-24 where Jesus says, "Woe to you, scribes and Pharisees, hypocrites! For you pay tithe of mint and anise and cummin, and have neglected the weightier matters of the law: justice and mercy and faith. These you ought to have done, without leaving the others undone. Blind guides, who strain out a gnat and swallow a camel!"

What would happen if we actually spent as much time ministering to people as we do trying to modify people's behavior? What if we focused less on trying to live like Christ lived (our version of his life anyway), and focused more on trying to love like he loved? We may find that while we may not succeed in changing a mind, we might possibly succeed at changing a heart, and therefore changing a life. In order to love on this level, it requires a certain level of honesty, the kind that is vulnerable and exposed. The kind of honesty that understands there is nothing to lose, but everything to gain. The kind of honesty that understands and empathizes because the person who holds it knows "it could've been me" … it should've been me … But, God intervened.

This kind of honesty can only come from a place of humility and reverence that says I am so undeserving of this grace that I would never try to withhold it from others. I have learned that people respect and appreciate leaders who walk in this level of honesty and transparency.

Back to my story: The following week I got married again, standing in my spiritual mother and father's living room one evening, with no ring, and only my mother to witness it. The following Sunday I stood before the congregation and confessed I was expecting a child and when. I told them I understood if any of them wanted to leave. Not a single member left. Instead, they encouraged me and told me they loved me. They told me they understand that I'm human and these things happen. In that moment, I felt the weight of my mistakes lift from my soul. I was the daughter redeemed. I was the prodigal son, even though I never left the pulpit … I had stepped away from my purpose. Yet, I was welcomed with open arms and being loved back to a place of purpose by my own congregation.

I do not believe this would've happened if they found out by some other means, if I hadn't confessed it out of my own mouth. Even still this was nothing but the mercy of God, it doesn't make me some kind of super saint. Getting married just because I was pregnant wasn't a great choice either. I paid a heavy price for that decision. This man cheated on me for nearly our entire marriage. I stayed with him because I felt obligated to make it work. I felt like I had to be the example and that I couldn't be a pastor and get a divorce. I stayed through the unthinkable because we had children together. Over the course of the marriage I lost myself, I even began to question my calling and sat down from ministry multiple times. I was traumatized by a marriage of habitual infidelity, lies, destruction, and deceit.

I hated him and I hated myself. I was that one sitting outside his baby mama's house at 4:00am looking at his car, thinking about knocking on the door. I was the one cleaning up bad checks he wrote on my bank account. I was the one visiting him in jail and bailing him out … over and over. I was the one who almost caught a charge behind this nigga when I found out he had a whole separate apartment on the other side of town and beat down his baby mama. I was the one with—not one, but two—DSS cases for Domestic Violence incidents that took place in the presence of our children. I was the one scratching "Liar … Cheater … Thief" in the side of his car. I was now that one showing up to church acting like everything was ok, not speaking and not sleeping in the same bed. Maybe this was karma. Now I understand why she stayed … there is a such a thing as toxic hope. Waking up every day hoping things will be different but knowing it will be the same. Too invested to walk away and too broken to stay at the same time, literally suspended in time between brokenness and bondage.

I ministered with a broken heart for the past 8 years and poured from an all-too-often empty vessel, and still God moved. People still got saved. People still got baptized. We still reached the community. Great things still happened. And that's the problem. We get lured into thinking we are OK, when the bottom line is God is doing it for his name's sake!

Imagine what he could do if I was whole? If you were whole? If we could keep it real with ourselves? I am writing this book for everyone from the pulpit to the pew because this is real for so many people. And the truth of the matter is too often the greatest level of brokenness, bondage, and bitterness is standing in the pulpit! It's time out for acting like it's all good when it's really all grace that hasn't exposed the hidden places in our lives where we've allowed brokenness, bitterness, and bondage to manifest in ways unacceptable to God and damaging to his Church.

On the third try, I finally got up the strength and nerve to go through with the divorce, which was finalized the same year I first wrote this book. I'm going to put it to you like Paul did in 1 Corinthians 15:9-10 when he said "I am the least of the apostles ... But by the grace of God, I am what I am: and his grace which was bestowed upon me was not in vain." So many times, we want to give "cute" testimonies about how God brought us out or through something, but we want to leave out how we contributed to the predicament or the not-so-holy parts of the story. And this is a big issue in the church, being fake. We are so busy keeping up appearances that we don't notice when our slip is showing. But the world does. And this is exactly why so many people, especially the younger generations, find themselves saying "See, that's why I don't go to church." And it's because there's more integrity on display in the world than in the church right now.

I believe before God exposes us to the world, he will give us an opportunity to correct course. By the time there is a public scandal concerning matters of the church, the leaders have ignored several opportunities to repent and reconcile with God in private. God has no issue with shaking the foundations of his church to reveal who was sent, who went, and who flat out needs to repent.

I am baring my soul, and by doing so, I hope to help someone to not make the mistakes I've made. The truth is always in order, even when it doesn't make us look good. At the end of the day, I know who I am, and whose I am. People can love it, hate it, take it, or leave it.

Either way, it is God who sits on the throne as our only judge. None of us are worthy. And thank God for Jesus … for it is by grace that we are saved—not of works, lest any of us should boast.

You know the scripture?
Psalm 105:15
"Touch not mine anointed
and do my prophets no harm."
That scripture was once used
to scare parishioners into being quiet,
doing the work, and questioning nothing.
It took me a while to realize that scripture
isn't just about pastors or leaders.
I'm God's anointed too. God also loves me.

PAULA MICHELLE GILLISON
WWW.LACKOFBETTER.COM

CHAPTER 4
P-VALLEY

WELCOME TO THE P.Y.N.K.

It's 2:48am on Sunday, December 13th, 2020. With 6 days left on the clock before this book is supposed to drop, I am binge watching P-Valley. The hit STARZ television series created by Katori Hall. First, let me just say she wrote the shit out this series! And as awesome as it is, I never would've watched it, not because it isn't good, but because I thought it was all about stripping. But if you can believe it, I was instructed to watch it by the Holy Spirit.

I was lying in bed agonizing about the release date for the book and feeling stressed about it not being done when I heard clear as day, "Welcome to the Pynk." I did a double-take in the Spirit and I heard it again … "Welcome to the Pynk." Anyone who has ever had their ancestors visit them in dreams or heard the voice of loved ones who have passed away know that God can speak in whatever voice he chooses. On this day, it was the voice of Nicco Annan, aka Uncle Clifford, the central character and staple of P-Valley.

Now listen, you don't have to believe a word you're reading, but if you can believe a virgin gave birth to the Savior through immaculate conception, this is small potatoes. I pulled up YouTube and searched

P-Valley reviews. I scrolled for a while and didn't find anything that spoke to me at first. Then I came up on it. A review of "Higher Ground", Season 1, Episode 3. In this episode we find Mercedes and Patrice Woodbine, a mother-daughter duo with an explosively dysfunctional relationship. Mercedes is a popular stripper at The Pynk and her mother is a faithful member of the church. Now, I'm not dropping the deets in this book because I'd rather you support the writers, actors, and staff by watching the show ... and make sure to put the chirren to bed before you get started.

What I will tell you is P-Valley is art imitating life. If you think it's about a strip club then you're not paying attention. The dysfunctional dynamic between Mercedes and her mother reflects that of countless PKs (preacher/pastor's kids). Parenting ain't easy, let alone preaching and parenting. But preachers always seem to demand a certain level of respect from their children that they are either unable or unwilling to reciprocate. I do not claim to be a psychologist or behavior specialist of any kind. I can only speak from my own experience and observation. In my personal opinion, so many pastors and preachers get it wrong at home when they place the burden on their children to choose between faith and fuckery. See, you thought I was about to get deep didn't you? This ain't deep! It's called integrity ... or lack thereof.

For so many PKs the closest example they have of God is their parents, and what they see on a daily basis is a two-faced, self-righteous, judgmental, unkind caricature of Christ. Far too often their parents are both conductors of pain and purveyors of purpose in their lives. Unfortunately, many aren't able to reconcile hurt and healing coming from the same vessel and end up walking away from the church, or even worse, God. When they finally walk away, they usually find more love, support, and respect in the streets than they ever did in the sanctuary.

I thought one of the most powerful scenes of P-Valley was in Episode 5 when Uncle Clifford, the strip club owner, comes to see Mercedes in jail after she and her mother ended up after having a knock-down, drag-out brawl (you gotta watch the show). Now, as a 6'2, cross-dressing, stiletto wearing, southern belle, country thug, Uncle Clifford is a sight to see at all times hunni! But in this particular scene, he is more of a mother to Mercedes than Patrice ... or "Bitchtrice" as he called her. He holds Mercedes by the face and encourages her to stay strong, and the way she looked up at Uncle Clifford like a lost little girl broke my heart. It is clear he loves Mercedes like his own daughter.

Not to be left out of the moment, here comes Patrice with venom in her mouth and says, "Well ain't that nice ... a visit from your pimp." It is Mercedes' response to her mother that I'm sure could come from the mouth of any number of PKs right this minute. Mercedes said, "My pimp? You should be the one to talk. That woman has done more for me in the last 7 years than you done a whole lifetime!" From there Mercedes goes on to drop an indictment of trifling acts her mother committed against her. In response to Mercedes, there is no apology. There is no contrition. There is no humility. Patrice responds to her daughter by saying, "God forgave me for that, you gon' have to forgive me for that too."

Patrice responds to Mercedes with an attitude and disposition as if to say you owe me forgiveness because God has forgiven me. I wonder how many PKs have forgiven their parents under duress. How many have forgiven as a survival mechanism rather than an act of faith or obedience to God? How many still carry the weight of their parents' transgressions on their soul? How many have anxiety walking into the church to this day behind the damage done to them in the name of Jesus?

The coldest part about it is these pastors get up Sunday after Sunday and preach wholeness, healing, and reconciliation to other families while simultaneously breaking, wounding, and ravaging their own. I don't know what it is about preachers and pastors that will have them neglect and reject their own children then turn around and instruct them to reject the world. If you reject them and they reject the world, where does that leave them? Instead of choosing to live in purgatory, many of them find solace in Places You Never Knew God existed that rescue, embrace, celebrate, encourage, and empower those rejected by the church.

So many of these pastors run their homes like the trap house and their churches like a brothel. "What happens in the house stays in the house" and their children are required to turn tricks every Sunday to validate their image. Everyone is expected to be polished up, fully present and playing their role. And for what? For the accolades, for the applause, for the approval of the congregation? Because it sure in the hell isn't for the souls, for the Savior, or for the Kingdom.

It's true that there are no perfect parents, but some pastors have forgotten they are parents to begin with and instead try to pastor their children, forcing their children to submit to their title and honor a position they barely honor themselves. They leave no room for their children to have their own identity because they're too busy exploiting the time, trust, and talent of their family to prop up their own identity.

In one scene on P-Valley Season 1, Episode 2, Sista Woodbine is calling Mercedes to check her about paying her tithes. First of all, if you EVA get a phone call about paying tithes, you need to leave that church, expeditiously. That is not of God. Patrice has her eyes set on the pulpit, and in an attempt to impress the pastor, she is using money her daughter makes stripping to pad the church's bank account. Yet, every chance she gets she has something sideways to say to Mercedes about her profession. And it is a profession. The straight up technical skill and strength with which these women murder that pole could very easily have them on tour with Cirque Du Soleil!

At one point Patrice says, "I can't believe I even let you hide your booty money in the church building fund." This. This right here is that bullshit. What you not gon' do is preach me into hell with your hands elbow-deep in my pockets! How the fuck you gon' judge me and use me?! How can you cash in on my gift and condemn me at the same time? And that is the problem with the church. Nothing is off limits and contrary to what they preach over these pulpits. Nothing is sacred. These pastors will gladly receive the gift and reject the giver. I am reminded of Tonex, currently known as B.Slade. I cannot think of another gospel artist more gifted during or after his time in the gospel arena. To this day, the power and impact of this man's gift is unmatched. If you have ever heard him then you know that his voice is literally liquid anointing! Everyone knew he was "different", but he tried to conform to the restraints of religion as long as he could. When he finally chose to walk unapologetically in his truth as someone who refuses to be confined by the religious and rigid rules of sexuality, the church straight up destroyed him.

After years of sangin' down the house and slaying in the Spirit every time he touched the mic, all of a sudden, he was an unfit vessel for the glory of God. The church and the gospel music industry stood back and watched this man crumble beneath the weight of the cross they crucified him with. They always knew who and what he was, but as long as he played by their rules, he could stay in the game. Until enough was enough, and one of the greatest Gospel artists to ever do it walked away from the church. He summed it up perfectly in his single "Change" when he said, "If this is too much for you to handle, I was always too much to handle … there ain't nothing new bout me, you don't want authenticity, you don't want sincerity, 2020 brought me clarity." This is just one example of how the church, and especially the Black Church, has slaughtered more sheep than the devil ever could.

I believe PKs sometimes have an extra helping of hell. Maintaining a healthy relationship with the church after growing up in the church is nothing short of a miracle. Many from all cultures and denominations are increasingly choosing to walk away from the church entirely. Not because they don't believe in God, but because they don't believe in the version of him the church is selling. They see more Christ in Uncle Clifford than they do in the Right Reverend Patrice Woodbine. They find more love, acceptance, and integrity where the so-called "thugs and thots" gather than they do in these pulpits and pews. Their freedom, their identity, and their lifestyle are not defined by the church. They've spent enough time incarcerated behind the bars of sermons unlived. They're done being used, abused, and manipulated.

If you cannot say the same, I hope this book empowers you to consider your exit strategy, because at some point these walls are coming down. I leave you with one piece of advice, courtesy of Uncle Clifford: "Rule No. 2—Always know where the exit's at up in this bitch, 'cause you never know when you got to turn a window into a door."

TRIGGERED

The American Psychiatric Association defines Post-traumatic Stress Disorder (PTSD) as "a psychiatric disorder that may occur in people who have experienced or witnessed a traumatic event such as a natural disaster, a serious accident, a terrorist act, war/combat, or rape or who have been threatened with death, sexual violence or serious injury." When we think of the term PTSD, we may default to military engagements, combat veterans or more blatantly traumatic events such as near-death experiences. However, it is my personal opinion that trauma has many levels, and anyone can experience a certain measure of PTSD as a result of any number of physical, mental, emotional, verbal, and yes, spiritual impact factors.

I am not a psychologist or a licensed counselor. I am simply someone who has lived long enough to go through some things. And when I look at the symptoms of PTSD, I see the evidence of it in my own life, and maybe you do as well. The symptoms of those who are diagnosed with PTSD vary, but fall closely within 4 categories:

1. **Intrusion:** Intrusive thoughts such as repeated, involuntary memories; distressing dreams; or flashbacks of the traumatic event.

2. **Avoidance:** Avoiding reminders of the traumatic event may include avoiding people, places, activities, objects and situations that may trigger distressing memories.

3. **Alterations in Cognition and Mood:** Negative thoughts and feelings leading to ongoing and distorted beliefs about oneself or others (e.g., "I am bad," "No one can be trusted"); Ongoing fear, horror, anger, guilt or shame.

4. **Hyperarousal and Reactivity:** Symptoms may include being irritable and having angry outbursts; behaving recklessly or in a self-destructive way; being overly watchful of one's surroundings in a suspecting way; being easily startled; or having problems concentrating or sleeping.

I understand that enduring years of drama, chaos, and confusion in church may not qualify as a "traumatic event" but many have certainly had experiences that would qualify. Have you ever thought about something and gotten angry all over again like it just happened? And don't let it happen early in the day because then you have to spend the whole day trying to recover from a thought! I sometimes think back to the night I was on my back in the backseat of my pastor's car and wonder how different my life would be if that never happened. Even when I was pastoring, I don't attend many church services, because after all these years I still have a bad taste in my mouth about church, and although it has eased up over time, it hasn't disappeared entirely. When I meet a preacher I'm automatically on guard, looking and listening for the angle. When I meet a First Lady, I'm automatically wondering what's really going on at home, I wonder if her smile is real.

I have trained myself to accommodate outwardly what I detest and reject inwardly. It's like I'm fighting a gag reflex in the Spirit every time I step foot in a church. Even when I'm the one speaking, there's the excitement of the Word inside me and the opportunity to express it, but, at the same time, there's also disdain for the entire process that brought me to the stage. The pomp and circumstance, the traditions and rituals, the positions and platitudes, idle conversations and clichés, the competition and judgment ... all of which I can tolerate if I feel like there's something God would have me to say. But there are some who can't even bring themselves to the thought of coming to church, let alone actually walking through the doors.

For a growing number of people church has become a trigger. The trauma they experienced at the hands of those who were supposed to be representing God is just too much. The pain they can't un-feel, the words they can't un-hear, the events they can't un-see on a replay reel in their souls won't let them leave the church even though they left a long time ago. So, they believe in God, and possibly Jesus, but refuse to call themselves Christians. They don't trust anything that has anything to do with the church. According to them no preachers can be trusted, they all shady. I see them on Facebook debating about whether there really is a God ... whether we're the real Jews ... whether we should call ourselves Hebrews ... whether the Bible is just a historic tool of Anglo-European oppression used to enslave black minds ... and maybe it was ... but what they used it for doesn't define what it is.

You can poison someone to death over time with arsenic, but that's not what the Creator intended. Arsenic is a natural component of the earth's crust existing throughout the environment in air, water, and land. In its organic form it poses little to no threat to humans. But in its inorganic form—pesticides, metal adhesives, wood preservatives, ammunitions and other forms created through industrial processes, it is a carcinogen (cancer-causing substance) deadly to humans. According to the World Health Organization inorganic arsenic is the most significant chemical contaminant in drinking-water globally. The greatest threat to public health from arsenic originates from contaminated groundwater. In other words, it is extracted from the earth in its organic form, chemically altered, used for the purposes of man, returned to the earth as a poison, then consumed by the people.

This is a perfect analogy of the church. Something real and naturally existing has been perverted for profit and fed back to the people as poison.

The problem is some of those who have rejected Christ and the church realize the water is tainted but can't see the Source for looking at the saints. They know God is real in their heart, but the reflex is to reject the Gospel and anyone preaching it. They've felt the presence of God, but perhaps not when they believed they needed him the most. They have suffered mentally, emotionally, physically and spiritually as a direct result of their proximity to the church, which some interpret as Acts of God. Their entire concept of God and faith is shaped by their trauma. They simply cannot reconcile what they have experienced with who he is.

This term doesn't exist in the medical community, but I call it Post Traumatic Spiritual Disorder. All the symptoms are the same, and just like Post Traumatic Stress Disorder, most of those who suffer from it don't know they have it. It took me a long time to realize I was suffering from spiritual PTSD. The initial trauma compounded by years of micro-traumas have tainted my relationship with God and the church. Over years the well has been poisoned, and once the well is poisoned so is everything drawn from it.

So many souls are thirsty and searching for living water. So many souls are hungry and seeking the living bread. They come to the church hoping to drink and be fed only to be served tainted meals on dirty dishes with bad customer service. Those who realize they are being poisoned either separate themselves from the church and pursue God … or separate themselves from God and reject the church. All I can say is I understand. And I believe God does as well.

If you're reading this and you've separated yourself from God on any level as a result of church hurt, please let this book be your invitation directly from the Father to try the Source. God is not what they did. God is not what they said. Forgive God for not showing up when you thought he should. Forgive God for not answering the prayer. Forgive God for letting you go through that. Forgive God for allowing it to happen. Please forgive the God you thought he was and give yourself permission to try and see the God he is.

*Loving Jesus doesn't always
cure suicidal thoughts.
Loving Jesus doesn't always cure PTSD.
Loving Jesus doesn't always cure anxiety.
But that doesn't mean that Jesus
doesn't offer us companionship and comfort.
He always does that.*

JARRID WILSON
PASTOR AND MENTAL HEALTH ADVOCATE

CHAPTER 5
THE SUNKEN PLACE

IT'S NOT YOU, IT'S ME

I was searching for a place where I could simply worship in peace. I tried returning to Redemption a few times, but after serving in smaller ministries it just felt too impersonal. It was too much and not enough at the same time. I don't remember who invited me, but in 2007 I started attending a small, start-up church in Greenville. It was a recent church plant from another local ministry, pastored by a husband and wife team. They were truly good people. It was refreshing to finally be part of a ministry that didn't look like the set of Maury Povich every other Sunday. Once again, I began to serve as the youth pastor and was being trained in ministry and outreach.

The teaching was great, the people were nice, and I was given increasingly more responsibility in the church. One summer the pastors went on vacation and instructed me to bring the message that Sunday. I was so nervous, I remember studying furiously, taking meticulous notes and even designing a PowerPoint. I wanted to make them proud. The Sunday came, and I remember trembling in the pulpit. My family had come to hear me speak. I had invited my boss from work, and she actually came! I was beyond nervous, scared to death I was going to bomb this thing. I managed to settle myself and get started. I remember the entire room being quiet as I ministered. Aside from a few grunts and amens, it seemed like I was preaching a funeral. I couldn't wait to get to the end. I finally wrapped up, the praise team closed the service, and all I could think was how terrible the sermon had been.

But something amazing happened. People swarmed me and began to tell me how awesome the message was. I was shocked! My boss came up to me and said this was one of the best messages she had ever heard. I was floored, and I still couldn't believe it. I thought maybe they were just being kind. So I responded, "Really?! I couldn't tell, everyone was so quiet, I thought you were all bored to death." Her response changed my perspective about church and preaching from that day forward. She said, "I was listening. I didn't want to miss anything." At that moment, I realized I had been conditioned to believe that screaming, shouting, and constant noise was what it meant to "have church." I was so used to performance preaching and theatrics that I misinterpreted the silence as an indictment against my ability to deliver the Word effectively.

The truth of the matter is, we should question a worship experience where everyone is jumping, shouting, and constantly yelling back at the preacher. There's nothing wrong with saying Amen and having a good time in church, but at some point, we have to wonder whether we're actually getting anything out of it. Are we really seeking God and his Word or just showing up in church clothes to clap for our favorite Sunday morning quarterback? Are we really being edified or showing up to the set of The Real Housewives—Church Edition? Are we showing up Sunday after Sunday to "do it for the vine" or actually seeking, serving, and living for the vine? I'm convinced the vast majority of churches are nothing more than social clubs offering weekly concerts, gimmick-filled motivational speeches, and guilt-filled fundraisers.

It became apparent to me then, and moreso now, that I am called to teach. Not only am I called to teach, but I am called to teaching, which may be one of the reasons I was attracted to this ministry in the first place. These pastors were great teachers, but after a while my relationship with them began to shift. I was growing into the gift of discernment and what some may call prophecy. I knew the Word of God but was ignorant in the ways of the Spirit. Because of that, my gift was on point, but I was out of order. It's one thing to be knowledgeable, but wisdom is an entirely separate matter.

I began to pick up on things in the Spirit, and instead of seeking God concerning what he was showing me, and what I should do with the information I was given, I'd make flesh moves ... flex moves. If you're in the church, you know what I mean. I would tell people their business, call people out, and share things God showed me about someone with others. Right now, there are prophets making flesh moves in pulpits, on tv, and on social media. Some of them aren't hearing from God at all, like a few prominent false prophets who wrongly predicted the outcome of the most recent presidential election in the United States. Then there are those who are in fact hearing from the Holy Spirit but are operating out of order. They are speaking when they should be silent. They are preaching when they should be praying. They are rebuking people publicly who they should be admonishing privately. I know it when I see it because it used to be me.

God began to show me some things concerning my pastors at the time, and instead of me praying about it, I told them about it.

Needless to say, they weren't very receptive. In addition to this, I was feeling a great pull in the spirit to start my own ministry. I was being encouraged to do so by people who heard me teach, inside and outside of the church I was attending. I had one couple attending the same church tell me, the only reason we're still here is we're waiting for you to start your church.

All of this sounds very flattering, but if you're not well-grounded in God and seasoned with humility it can quickly go to your head. I started making plans to start my own church, while I was still attending this church, and told some of the members about it. The pastors found out and confronted me about it. They were gentle in their approach, but basically accused me of trying to steal their members. I told them that wasn't my intent, but looking back at that situation, I can see why their accusation was somewhat legitimate. The problem was I had outgrown their ministry. What I failed to realize is that while I had outgrown the content, I had not outgrown their care. It was true that I no longer felt like I was being fed, the material just wasn't mature enough for my spiritual palate, but I misappropriated an important opportunity to hone my craft, build my character, and learn to submit and serve leadership for a season.

I believe I was placed by God at that ministry to be trained in the art and heart of pastoral care, which these two had in spades. It was clear that I was called to pastor, but I squandered their trust by leaving prematurely and not involving them in the launch of my ministry. At this point, you may be wondering why I included this in the book. I could not write a book about church hurt and skip over the fact that many preachers and pastors are hurt by their members as well. So many times, pastors pour everything they have into the people, only for some of those same people to turn around and stab them in the back, speak ill of their ministries, or take everything they've learned and launch out without even so much as a thank you to the platform that helped them get there. I was deeply convicted by the way I left that ministry and eventually went back to ask their forgiveness and apologize for the way I left, which they were graceful enough to accept.

In order to justify my exit, I made them the problem. Instead of simply saying, "this is no longer the place for me," I felt the need to minimize their capacity to cover me. When in reality they had done everything God instructed them to do concerning me. They were not the problem. I was the problem. I was not mature enough to serve in second knowing I believed I was called to be first. I was not humble enough to be cared for thinking I was called to care for others. I was too impatient to be still and be equipped because I was called to equip others. I knew plenty about God's word but was woefully unlearned in his ways.

I'm not proud of this part of my journey, but I can honestly say I took this lesson to heart and I believe I'm a better person because of it. I know I'm not the only one who can identify with this, especially those who feel extremely gifted in their call. On either side of the matter, there are those who are not settled enough in their gift to allow it to use them to glorify God, and instead they are using the gifts of God to glorify themselves. They are caught up in pride and self-importance. They are addicted to the accolades and applause. They're getting high on their own supply and are ignorantly, or knowingly, burning bridges that God built to bring them into a greater place of purpose. And to them I can affirm Proverbs 16:18 from experience: "Pride goes before destruction, And a haughty spirit before a fall." If you feel convicted in any way reading this, maybe it's you. If so, you should pray and ask God how to make it right, and then be obedient to the instruction of the Holy Spirit.

If you're on the receiving end of this, decide right now that you will not take this personally, because it's not personal. Release the disappointment and bitterness of betrayal to God, because their offense is against him, not you or your ministry. You must do what you encourage others to do, and that is to forgive them and pray for their deliverance as they find their way to purpose. Your ability to lead was never based on their acknowledgement of your capacity to cover them, but it may have been limited by the content of their character and their willingness to submit to God.

Resist the natural urge to close your heart to the people. Reject the notion that it's not worth it, because it is. I'm reminded of the ten lepers Jesus healed in Luke 17:11-19. The scriptures say Jesus was on his way to Jerusalem, and as he was going into a village, ten men who had leprosy met him and called out to him to have pity on them. When he saw them, he instructed them to go and show themselves to the priests. Let's pause for a moment and look at this a bit closer … first of all, Jesus was already on his way to Jerusalem before he encountered these guys. That means they were just part of the process on his way to purpose. He didn't call out to them … they called out to him. Why is this important? Whoever shows up at your church or seeks you out for mentorship and cover must first acknowledge that you have something they need. Their presence at your ministry is their version of the lepers' cry.

Just like Jesus, when you see them you do what comes naturally = you instruct them. The instructions they received were a prescription for a miracle. The scriptures say, "as they went, they were cleansed." In other words, there was a tangible and undeniable impact on their lives as a direct result of the instruction they received from Christ. But check this out. Out of ten lepers, only one returned to thank Christ and give God praise. One. And that one was a Samaritan! I ain't got time to deal with that, just know this dude wasn't even in the clique! Jesus said, "Were not all ten cleansed? Where are the other nine? Has no one returned to give praise to God except this foreigner?" Take Notes! The ones closest to you might be the last ones to acknowledge you! One out of ten. That means 9 times out of 10 this is going to be a thankless job.

As a pastor I've said "they can go to hell" a few times and was talking about church folks! That's because I took their actions personally and their offense to heart. But it's never about the 9 or the 1. It's always about The One. Give it to God and understand that whatever you gave to them came from God, they don't owe you anything. It doesn't matter who stays or goes, or what "they say" when they get there.

Release yourself from the need to hear a thank you, or the need for them to reach back and give you props. We are serving "as unto the Lord." Keep in mind that, above all else, we have been called to love. And in the words of my friend Michele Oney Snyder, "If you really want to love the broken, be prepared to bleed."

OUT OF THE DARKNESS

Within just the last 2 years there has been report after report of pastors committing suicide. An Illinois pastor, overcome with grief following the death of his wife, shot himself in front of his mother and son after stating he was hearing his wife's voice and footsteps. A Georgia pastor was found by his wife in the driveway of their home with a self-inflicted gunshot wound. He killed himself in between

Sunday services. A rising megachurch pastor, author and mental health advocate died by suicide at only 30 years old, after preaching and ministering consistently about depression and mental health. A Missouri megachurch pastor with multiple satellite churches in South Carolina committed suicide this past May. I could go on, but the point is, mental health is severely mismanaged, unaddressed, and overlooked in the church.

Church folks have a way of dismissing the mental health crisis as a lack of faith or some type of spiritual bondage. While it may be true that there could be a spiritual aspect to mental wellness, you can only pray so much before you actually need to look beyond the church for an answer. If these pastors, full of faith and light, still found themselves in a place of darkness, how much more susceptible are the souls in the pews?

This may strike you as blasphemous, but Christ is not the cure for everything, and the Bible is not the answer to all bondage. Being saved and attending church is not a magical shield against the complexities of the human mind.

I cannot tell you how many times I've battled depression and stood in the pulpit spreading the Gospel of hope while feeling hopeless, preaching peace while void of any semblance of it in my personal life, and encouraging others to love, with hate and bitterness in my heart. There were days I didn't even want to get out of bed, let alone stand in front of a congregation and preach. There were times when I counseled the broken while I was breaking, tended the wounds of the people while I was bleeding, and poured out to the pews from the emptiness and isolation of the pulpit. I buried myself in the church and the issues of others in the name of ministry. And for all the scripture that

I read and the prayers that I prayed I still couldn't shake the mental, emotional, and spiritual heaviness that comes from depression.

The church is so bent on making faith, or lack thereof, a cure-all for all of life's trials and tribulations, they leave those struggling with mental health to suffer alone in the shadows ... or in the pulpit ... to fend for themselves. While most are too ashamed to reach out for fear of being trivialized or given the same old tired counsel to "trust God everything's gonna be alright" just "pray about it" or even worse, being blamed for how you're feeling, and being accused of a secret sin or some unforgiveness that you need to repent for, or perhaps some demonic oppression that you need to be delivered from that must be the source of your torment.

The church seems to place the entire burden of mental wellness on your ability to truly believe God is the answer, and if so, you should be able to pray and fast your way out of anything. I believe this is especially true in the "black church" because culturally we generally don't make room for mental health. We don't discuss it in our community or provide safe space for those who struggle with mental health. Historically, we've had to survive, and we handle every aspect of life in survivor-mode with a "get over it" and "ain't nobody got time for that" attitude that has crossed over into the church.

As a creative I feel like we have a double burden beyond the church experience to constantly express "good vibes" and encourage or empower others even when we're feeling powerless. Creatives in the church may be among those who struggle the most with mental health, but they break so beautifully that people celebrate their gift and totally miss the queues and cries for help subtly evident in their art. If you were anywhere near a television in 2020, and most likely you were directly in front of one for the better part of the year, then you may have witnessed the short-lived presidential run of Kanye West. During one of his rallies here in South Carolina he appeared to have a very public mental breakdown. The insults, jokes, and memes were ruthless, but many of the same folks were praising the release of his gospel album a few months prior.

Kanye West is a creative genius, who happens to be a celebrity, but what he's going through is not unique. Many of us have people in our own families and circles who have weathered the same storm. But if you're not a billionaire with a global platform it goes unspoken of. Especially in the black community where mental health issues are considered a weakness. The church in general didn't seem receptive to Kanye West in the first place. I didn't see many posts calling for prayer and intercession, but he was invited to perform at these megachurches to suit their purpose and quickly discarded afterward. I'm not talking about Kanye West in an attempt to whitewash him or advocate for his brand. I just find it so agitating and hypocritical that church folks pick and choose certain issues and people who deserve empathy and honor, while others aren't worthy of our compassion or consideration.

On any given Sunday, there are people sitting in the congregation who are battling depression, struggling with mental health, or have considered or attempted suicide, including the pastor. Yet, very few churches offer suicide counseling or mental wellness ministries. What's worse is many churches teach that people who commit suicide are going to hell. I don't understand how anyone who reads the Scriptures could come to this conclusion. One flimsy explanation I've heard is the person is going to hell because they committed murder and didn't ask for forgiveness before they died. Ok, let's go with this logic for a moment. The Merriam-Webster dictionary defines suicide as "performing a deliberate act resulting in the voluntary death of the person who does it". Let's put aside for a moment what we know or imagine when we hear the word "Suicide" and deal strictly with the description—Suicide is a deliberate act resulting in voluntary death.

If we agree with this definition, then every smoker who has damaged their lungs and given themselves emphysema or lung cancer should Go To Hell. Every drug addict who damaged their hearts and died or overdosed should Go To Hell. Every Alcoholic who ruined their liver and killed themselves with cirrhosis should Go To Hell. Every Obese Person who is Eating themselves to death and dying of self-inflicted COPD, High Blood Pressure, and Diabetes should go straight to Hell. Why? Because every last one of them killed themselves. Outside of what they did to their own bodies they may still be alive.

We don't wanna send Big Momma to Hell after the doctor told her to change her eating habits, she didn't, then died accordingly... no no no … Big Momma is going to heaven right? But if in a state of total hopelessness and untreated depression some poor soul hangs themselves oh my, now that … that right there is unforgivable? Zero Grace for that person because they didn't "ask for forgiveness" … but Big Momma who died of a stroke due to high blood pressure because she literally ate herself to death, she does not have to ask forgiveness … she's going straight to Heaven right? Why does Big Momma get a free pass? Why does your Newport smoking uncle who also happens to be a deacon at the church get a free pass? This is the Surgeon General's warning on the back of a pack of cigarettes:

SURGEON GENERAL'S WARNING: Smoking Causes Lung Cancer, Heart Disease, Emphysema, and May Complicate Pregnancy. SURGEON GENERAL'S WARNING: Quitting Smoking Now Greatly Reduces Serious Risks to Your Health.

This is literally a pre-printed suicide note for anyone who smokes cigarettes. If suicide means to engage in a deliberate act that you know could or will kill you, why isn't smoking cigarettes punishable by eternal hell fire? The only difference between smoking cigarettes and swallowing pills is an immediate vs. gradual death, but it's all suicide.

Now let me really screw with your theology for a minute. Jesus said in John 10:11, "I am the good shepherd. The good shepherd gives his life for the sheep," and goes on to say in Verse 17 and 18, "Therefore My Father loves Me, because I lay down My life that I may take it again. No one takes it from Me, but I lay it down of Myself. I have power to lay it down, and I have power to take it again. This command I have received from My Father." In other words, Jesus literally came to earth on a suicide mission. He voluntarily engaged in an act that he knew would result in his death, yet these so-called saints don't see the irony in sending someone to hell who commits suicide. Not only does this reasoning have no foundation in scripture, but it is also fatally flawed logically. Equating mental illness, clinical depression, or abject hopelessness to faithlessness, sin, and separation from God is utterly contrary to the nature of God, a God who defines himself as Love.

Committing suicide does not indicate a lack of faith in God, but a lack of faith in self. The lack of hope and ability to see yourself in any other state of being than you are at that moment, to the point that you are convinced that death is better than existing in your current condition. I have experienced too much Grace and Mercy to believe I serve a God who sees hopelessness as wickedness. Since we don't have a Heaven or Hell to put people in then I would suggest we stop trying to sit in God's Seat, using God's Word to direct traffic to either location as if we, in our fickle and finite human ability, have the capacity to determine the eternal destination of the balance of souls held completely and only in the hands of God.

Any church or pastor teaching that suicide is an unforgivable act resulting in eternal condemnation does not know God nor his word, and as far as I'm concerned can go straight to hell themselves. Not only have they demonized a child of God but placed the burden and thought of that soul being unredeemable on the heart of the loved ones they left behind. Suicide is not an act against God, it is an act against Self. In my opinion it is the result of a broken heart, broken mind, broken soul, and broken spirit. Last I checked the God I serve isn't sending folks to hell for brokenness. Anyone who thinks he is, doesn't know him.

The scriptures are very clear about what God considers an unpardonable sin. During one of the many dust-ups between Jesus and the scribes and pharisees (church folk), the scribes accused Jesus of being demon possessed, and claim the reason he was able to cast out demons is because he has been empowered by the "ruler of demons" to do so. Jesus responded to this allegation in Mark 3:28-29 by saying, "Assuredly, I say to you, all sins will be forgiven the sons of men, and whatever blasphemies they may utter; but he who blasphemes against the Holy Spirit never has forgiveness, but is subject to eternal condemnation."

Not only is suicide not included in this very short list of unforgiveable sins, Christ says "all sins will be forgiven" the sons of men ... did you catch that?! And check this out, the one unpardonable sin is "Blaspheme against the Holy Spirit." The Billy Graham Evangelistic Association describes it as "a refusal to accept the witness of the Holy Spirit to who Jesus was and what he had come to do." Another Bible commentary states, "To commit this sin one must consciously, persistently, deliberately, and maliciously reject the testimony of the Spirit." I don't know about you but seems to me the preachers and pastors who refuse to accept the fullness of who Jesus is and what he came to do, are closer to going to hell than a person who ends their own life.

The issue is we make the mistake of thinking people who commit suicide need to be forgiven to begin with. (I know that will shake some folks' theology). A lot of "saved" people have committed suicide, and guess what, their souls were secure before the act; not because of what they did to themselves, but because of Who they confessed to believe in. According to the scriptures, committing suicide does *not* cancel your confession of faith in God. "God knows my heart", is something we love to say when we're cutting up, but it is true. God's grace and mercy are so much bigger than we could ever imagine, and apparently much bigger than some saints can accept.

To all the hyper-religious folks going to and fro seeking whom you may devour, be careful that you don't find yourself in the place you've designated for others. Think about this ... a sinner dying on the cross next to Jesus said "Remember me when you come into your kingdom," to which Jesus replied, "Truly I say to you, today you shall be with Me in Paradise." This was a criminal who neither knew nor acknowledged Christ until he was dying as a result of his own sin on the cross. In that moment, he received grace from God before Jesus died and rose again. So apparently God had prepared Grace for him, and it wasn't even tied to the resurrection of Christ! My goodness what kind of love is that!? Are we to believe that a dying criminal can be saved over 2,000 years ago while Jesus was still a man on the cross, but someone who is broken today doesn't have access to the greater grace made available after that same Jesus graduated from the cross to the right hand of the Father? I think not! I could be wrong … but I think more highly of my God than to believe that he would respond to brokenness, hopelessness, and mental illness with fire and brimstone.

For those who have lost a loved one to suicide, do not let your heart be troubled, their soul belongs to God. Be at peace in knowing God knows the heart. Psalm 34:18 says, "The Lord is close to the brokenhearted and saves those who are crushed in spirit." We serve a God who loves us beyond measure, we cannot even imagine the expanse of his grace. Release that weight to God, do not carry it another day. Forgive yourself for not knowing. Forgive yourself for not understanding. Forgive yourself for not being there. Forgive yourself for not saving them. That was never your job. You have not failed them. God knows the day and the hour for each of us, and his grace is sufficient.

If you are in leadership, please make time for your own mental health and spiritual wellness. You don't owe it to anyone to continue serving from a place of brokenness. We often use the term "stepping down" when a pastor decides to step away from the pulpit, but this suggests a demotion from an elevated place. However, every place you occupy is a place of purpose. We don't consider changing a flat tire a scandal. It's necessary to pull over and change it in order to continue. Likewise, there is no shame in stepping aside to heal, to recover, to refocus, and to realign your relationship with God.

It's easy for leadership to step into savior-mode, but we are not saviors, and we are not superhuman. We are simply humans who serve an extraordinary God, a God who wants us whole. If you are struggling with depression or suicidal thoughts, please know that you are loved, your presence in this Earth is appointed by God and you have purpose. Please don't sacrifice your future to your past or present. Don't give up on your tomorrow today. Hold on, your latter shall be greater! It doesn't matter if you've lost everything. God can do more with what you have left than what you started out with, even if all you have left is you. There's nothing you did yesterday or today that's worth cancelling your tomorrow.

Sometimes it's darker with your eyes open than closed, but one thing I know for certain, if you seek the light you will see the light. You don't have to suffer in silence, you are not alone. Reach out and talk to someone, call the National Suicide Hotline, someone is available 24 hours a day at (800) 273-8255. Refuse to believe the lie that nobody understands, because God does. Refuse to believe that ending it all is the only answer.

Give yourself a chance, you are worth it.

*Jesus's teaching consistently attracted
irreligious while offending the
Bible-believing religious people of his day.
However, our churches do not
have this same effect,
which can only mean one thing.
Our preaching and practices are not
declaring the same message that Jesus did.*

TIM KELLER

CHAPTER 6
SHAKE THE DUST

THE PENIS AND THE PULPIT

I spent hours studying biblical accounts of women in ministry. I researched articles and publications that align with what I know. I sought out historical figures to present like show and tell. I reached for voices that would affirm my own. I almost took the bait. This chapter almost became a theological dissertation of apologetic exegesis. But in this moment, as I write these words, I just became aware of who I Am. If the fruit doesn't explain it then you don't want to understand.

Who am I that I should attempt to justify the indiscriminate distribution of the Holy Spirit as if God's Word requires vindication? Who are these so-called saints that have the audacity to put a restriction on the flow of the anointing? Who are these traffic police, mall cops, and self-appointed security guards of the Gospel? Which one of you have elevated chromosomes above the agenda of the Creator? Where were you when God formed me in the womb? How dare you stand at the entrance of an empty tomb and disqualify the voice and vessel that brought you!

I see them coming a mile away. They have convinced themselves that their robes and collars mean something. Their chins tilted at the exact angle of false humility. Creases sharp as the edges of the cross in their left pocket. These muthafuckas think they something. What is it about the combination of a penis and a pulpit that elevates their opinion of themselves? What I don't understand is how in the world you can read the Word of God … preach the Word of God … and still have your ass on your shoulders like your shit don't stink? If you really read what's in that Book, it'll make you humble. To know that there's nothing at all you can do to earn the love of the Good, Good Father, but He's steady loving us anyway.

So many are searching for that love too. Looking for his voice like I was. Seeking a certain affirmation that can only come from a father's presence. I was 13 when I met him, 14 when he groomed me, 18 when he fucked me, 19 when I married him, and 23 when I divorced him … this man locked down a decade of my life and it began with a penis and a pulpit. If I had a dollar for every so-called preacher that came at me sideways since I was sixteen, I'd be wealthy. I don't know when it happened, but at some point, the pulpit became a symbol and extension of the male anatomy. And that's not even the worst part. How is it that these men will preach you into a place of purpose only to deny you access to it?

I came across an article earlier this year about a bit of controversy that sprang up over some comments made by world renowned pastor and author John MacArthur. This guy got a whole bible named after himself, so just try to understand the weight and level of influence he has built up over the last 30–40 years. At a conference in California he was asked by one of the panelists to give a brief response to what was supposed to be a one-word statement. Which actually turned out to be two words: Beth Moore. His direct response was "Go home." He then made more comments about there being no foundation for women preachers in Scripture. Then, as if that wasn't asinine enough, his assistant, Phil Johnson, said what comes to mind when he hears her name is "Narcissist," and cites Beth Moore as an example of what it means "to preach yourself rather than Christ." Now, I know John MacArthur is supposed to be some great theologian and maybe even considered to be some kind of present-day Apostle walking this earth, and I don't know who his little sidekick is, but I got one question for both of them. Who the fuck made ya'll the gatekeepers of the Gospel?

How insecure do you have to be to gather a bunch of men in a room so you can talk about how women aren't called to preach? Any man that spends any time talking about what God hasn't called a woman to do has lost sight of what he is called to do. These guys are sitting on a panel of old men, in a room full of men, talking to themselves in an echo chamber of little dicks and egos, while these Women of God are out here slaying for the Kingdom like the bosses they are. Women like Beth Moore, Priscilla Shirer, Joyce Meyer, Jasmin Sculark, Sheryl Brady and Sarah Jakes Roberts are speaking to crowds of thousands. Not only are they watering the hearts and souls of those thirsting for righteousness, they are serving the kingdom with global ministries, international missions, and building up their communities through service and philanthropy. If you ever heard any one of these women speak, it is impossible to conclude that they are "preaching themselves instead of Christ." It takes the audacity of a true narcissist to witness the undeniable impact of women in ministry and attempt to define, demean, and demote the Spirit of the Living God down to a dick.

John MacArthur stood in a pulpit in November 2019 and preached a sermon titled "Does the Bible Permit Women to Preach?" From the video you can see hundreds, if not a couple thousand people in attendance. In the tradition of all self-important male clergy, he uses 1

Corinthians 14:33-35 as a foundation, which says, "Let your women keep silent in the churches, for they are not permitted to speak; but they are to be submissive, as the law also says. And if they want to learn something, let them ask their own husbands at home; for it is shameful for women to speak in church." He said that this scripture is an absolute prohibition on women speaking in church, then goes on to say that it is not only improper but disgraceful. Now, I could take time here to beat the brakes off his theology using the same Word he used, but this is not about to be theologically heavy, because I am not writing a book of apologetics for the church. I owe religion nothing and I have nothing to prove. This is my testimony. This is what I have experienced as a minister of the Gospel who also happens to be female.

It took a while for me to figure out that I have no business trying to defend myself. It finally dawned on me that the whole entire conversation is a distraction. If you don't believe women should preach the Gospel that's your problem not mine. The real question is, what is the motive behind disqualifying the vessel? At one point the disciples had a similar disposition toward those who weren't part of their "clique" and they brought the issue to Jesus. In Mark 9:38 the Apostle John said, "Teacher, we saw someone who does not follow us casting out demons in Your name, and we forbade him because he does not follow us." Now the first thing you notice is John believes that he has the authority to tell someone else what they can and can't do in the name of Jesus. In other words, he told them to "Go Home". But Jesus responded, "Do not forbid him, for no one who works a miracle in My name can soon afterward speak evil of Me. For he who is not against us is on our side. For whoever gives you a cup of water to drink in my name, because you belong to Christ, assuredly, I say to you, he will by no means lose his reward." Jesus was literally saying you're worried about the wrong thing! Here's where you got it twisted, they don't follow you, they follow me, because if they didn't, they wouldn't be able to cast out a devil in my name anyway! Furthermore, whatever they are doing for the kingdom in My name is worthy of a reward.

How can you read this gospel and fix your mouth to say "Go Home" in response to someone preaching the Good News?! But check this out, just before this conversation, if you go back a few scriptures, the disciples were having a pissing match about who was the greatest and Jesus had to school them on humility. And that, ladies and gentlemen, is what it's all about: pride. Wanting to find any reason to exalt oneself above another, even if you must use the word of God to do so. Damn the debate about women preaching and focus on the fact that this man, having a global platform, and the attention of thousands of men, women, and children in attendance that day, did not take time to preach on the goodness of the Lord, the grace and mercy available through Jesus Christ, or the joy, peace, and wholeness we find in the promises of God. A man who is already knocking at heaven's door at 81 years old, took an hour, 14 minutes, and 45 seconds of his life, to preach to the lost, broken, and weary, a tainted exegesis of patriarchal bullshit empty of any presence of the Holy Spirit.

There is nothing he offered in that "sermon" to the drug addict hoping to get delivered from the pain they are numbing. There is nothing he offered in that sermon to the couple who is struggling in their marriage. There is nothing he offered in that sermon to the young adult trying to find his or her identity in this world. There is nothing he offered in that sermon to the woman who is being abused at home. There is nothing he offered in that sermon to bring light and purpose to someone buried beneath depression and contemplating suicide.

I bet MacArthur thought he accomplished something that day. Instead, he used his platform to prove a point instead of preaching the gospel. He used his congregation as a pawn in a ceremonious attempt to vindicate himself from the backlash of his flippant comments concerning Beth Moore.

I refuse to believe the God I serve instructed him to get up in front of all those people and tell them why women aren't called to preach. I refuse to believe the God I serve instructed him to get up in front of thousands and tell them women should be ashamed of preaching the Gospel. Again, I ask the question what is the motive? How does that benefit the Kingdom? If there was ever an example of somebody preaching themselves rather than Christ this is it!

The God I serve sent his son Jesus to the earth not only to shake, but to shatter every barrier between him and his own. And you mean to tell me that same God who spoke through an ass to give instructions to a man can't speak through a vagina? I pity the fool that doesn't think God won't use whoever he wants to use to get his word out. These preachers will stand in the pulpit and hold their entire congregation hostage to a self-serving, faithless message, while God has been in "Say I won't!" mode since the foundations of the earth.

One must ask why there would be such a great level of focus on minimizing the role of women in the church if it weren't already significant? The tired logic these pastors and preachers keep perpetuating is that somehow a woman preaching the Gospel usurps a man's headship. The premise assumes that a woman operating in her anointing equates to having authority over a man. This entire thought process wreaks of ignorance and insecurity. If you really believe God himself established man has the head, do you honestly believe a woman standing in a pulpit preaching the Gospel can do anything to destroy that order? I mean think about it, this logic literally suggests that a woman can wipe out the entire hierarchy of mankind, the social construct of God himself, by simply preaching the Gospel. Can you believe that shit?

Isaiah 61:1 declares, "The Spirit of the Lord God is upon me, Because the Lord has anointed me to preach good tidings to the poor; he has sent me to heal the brokenhearted, to proclaim liberty to the captives, and the opening of the prison to those who are bound." The same Spirit the Prophet Isaiah is speaking of is the same Spirit in Joel 2:28-29, "And it shall come to pass afterward that I will pour out my Spirit on all flesh; your sons and your daughters shall prophesy, your old men shall dream dreams, your young men shall see visions. And also on my menservants and on my maidservants I will pour out my Spirit in those days." And then, as if God knew the church would be slow to catch on, he repeated himself through the Apostle Peter in Acts 2:17–18, "And it shall come to pass in the last days, says God, that I will pour out of my Spirit on all flesh; your sons and your daughters shall prophesy, your young men shall see visions, your old men shall dream dreams. And on my menservants and on my maidservants I will pour out my Spirit in those days; and they shall prophesy." Are we really to believe what the Apostle Paul wrote in 1 Corinthians cancelled the words of the Prophet Isaiah, the Prophet Joel, and the Apostle Luke? Not at all. The word is to be taken as a whole, not chopped up into isolated pieces to suit the self-enriching purposes of arrogance and pride.

Now some will try to make a distinction between teaching and preaching, as did MacArthur, who attempted to throw out a funky ass caveat that women are called to teach, but they are called to teach other women. What I find amazing about any man that makes this argument, is how they deliberately choose to ignore the evidence in Scripture and in this common era, that women are in fact called to proclaim the Gospel to any who will receive it. Indulge me for a moment ... People will send their sons to school to be taught by female teachers, from preschool to Ivy League Universities, we send our sons to be taught by men and women, why? Because they are experts in their fields, or at minimum knowledgeable enough in the subject matter to teach it. We allow female teachers to instruct our sons because we are confident in their ability to do so. Yet, you have people in the church who will say a woman can teach your sons in Sunday school, but cannot preach the Gospel. Isn't it the same Word?

The same Word being taught in Sunday school is the same Word being taught in Sunday morning worship, just on an adult level. So, you're literally saying that women can teach boys, but not men? Or that they can teach men in all other places except the church? Let me ask this, what's the cutoff age? What is the cutoff age that a woman becomes disqualified to teach a man? Is it 12, 13 ... maybe 18? Yes, perhaps that's it, at 18 years old men immediately become the head and women automatically become unqualified to instruct them in the Gospel. When a boy turns 18 years old, maybe that's when a woman is no longer qualified to tell him anything that will help him to be a better man, a better husband, a better father, or a more committed man of God. Maybe after 18 years old there's nothing she can say to help him get free from drug addiction, nothing she can say to help him see how much Jesus loves him and that he doesn't have to live a life of defeat. She can educate him in college, she can train him at work, she can even instruct and prescribe medications as his physician, but about her preaching the Gospel to him ... now that is just downright shameful. Sounds petty doesn't it? Just as petty as someone saying a woman can teach but not preach ... funny how we try to split hairs over semantics and completely ignore the Scriptures.

So, I guess when God said I will pour out my spirit on *all* flesh, maybe that should be interpreted to mean just Men, something like how the founding fathers interpreted the constitution when they said "All men are created equal" but we know that didn't mean black men did it?

Later, the Letter of the Constitution was eventually fulfilled, after much bloodshed, civil war, and to this day ... we still fight for equality. I don't think it's surprising at all that there were a panel of old white men saying women can't preach or pastor. American Christianity has basically turned Jesus into a white, Republican man ... but that's a whole separate book by itself. At the end of the day, the fruit don't lie. You can tell an apple tree it's not an apple tree. You can have your panels of men giving all their theories and isolating scriptures to support their positions that the Apple Tree is clearly not an Apple Tree. You can have folks on these posts splice words and tell you your daughters can teach but they can't preach, as if there's a difference. I recall Jesus taught parables to bring the people to an understanding of the Gospel and the Kingdom. You can go on in your groups, cliques, and echo chambers proclaiming to each other how that Apple Tree is not an Apple Tree, meanwhile that Apple Tree is producing apples ... daily.

Souls are being saved, people are being delivered, orphanages and hospitals are being built, churches are being birthed, missions, revivals, crusades, and miracles are taking place ... meanwhile, back at the ranch, you've got a group of men, talking about how women aren't called to preach. To that I say, by all means you are entitled to your opinion. When we get to heaven, I'm sure God will sort it all out. In the meantime, we're going to win these souls by teaching and preaching the Gospel. The men and women who come to receive the Good News and choose to be encouraged and empowered by our ministries will continue to do so, why? Because we speak life, we speak truth, and we are called to do so.

If you don't agree, by all means, don't show up. But what no man can do is minimize, erase, ignore, or deny that souls are being saved, lives are being changed, communities are being impacted, missions are being carried out, families are being restored, and God is being glorified, because of what women are doing in and for the Kingdom. So, by all means continue this crusade against women preachers and pastors if it aids your purpose. Come together in your gatherings and sit on your panels, talking to each other about each other, measuring each other by each other, never inviting Christ into the conversation, while we continue to reach the world for Christ, and bear the fruit of the tree you say we're not. You don't own the Gospel. You don't have a monopoly on the Word of God. Your penis doesn't make you anymore qualified to spread the Good News, and if you believe that, then I would argue you could use a circumcision.

Women don't need your permission or approval to walk in the anointing of the true and living God. We know Whose team we're on. We don't follow you. We follow Jesus. The fruit is the only evidence necessary to define the tree. You can keep your pulpits … and your dusty-ass penises for that matter.

THE COUNTERFEIT VEIL

When Jesus died, the Scriptures say in Matthew 27:51 that "the veil of the temple was torn in two from top to bottom." From the top down, every barrier between God and mankind was destroyed. But somewhere along the way, we have allowed places and positions to reconstruct a counterfeit veil between God and his Church.

When I was pastoring some called me Pastor, some called me Prophetess, some called me Teacher, some called me Sister, and some called me Desimber. I was not offended. Why? Because my mother named me Desimber Rose Wattleton. None of these titles are on my birth certificate. I understand that God did not call us to positions in the Church, he called us to purpose in the Kingdom. It's acceptable to honor spiritual leaders, but we should never get offended when someone omits our title, as long as we're not omitting our purpose. The late Dr. Myles Munroe put it this way, "You can tell how effective you are as a leader by how many titles you get rid of."

These titles serve little purpose other than to set God's people apart from each other and to extend the distance between God and his church. Sometimes the people who have them make them more useless than they should be. They use these titles as status symbols for clout. They wear them with arrogance like some kind of accomplishment. Jesus called out the Sadducees and Pharisees for this kind of behavior in Mathew 23:6–12:

> "They love the best places at feasts, the best seats in the synagogues, greetings in the marketplaces, and to be called by men, 'Rabbi, Rabbi.' But you, do not be called 'Rabbi'; for One is your Teacher, the Christ, and you are all brethren. Do not call anyone on earth your father; for One is your Father, he who is in heaven. And do not be called

teachers; for One is your Teacher, the Christ. But he who is greatest among you shall be your servant. And whoever exalts himself will be humbled, and he who humbles himself will be exalted."

Not only has the church become infatuated with titles, but those who have them have exalted themselves above the people they are called to serve. I cannot tell you how many pastors I've come across that don't even like people. How can you claim to be a shepherd but despise the sheep? They do everything in their power to minimize personal interaction with their congregations. They surround themselves with an entourage of yes men, red tape, and "security." The only time you see them is when it's time for them to perform. They treat their congregations like fans at a concert and they are the main attraction. They place several layers between themselves and the people so they can avoid direct interaction if at all possible. Yet, we serve a Savior who made himself of no reputation, and took upon him the form of a servant, and was made in the likeness of men. We serve a Savior who did everything he could to get closer to the people in order to maximize our access to the Father. If anyone is deserving of this honor, it is Jesus, yet you will not find even one scripture where Jesus asked, told, or required anyone to call him anything other than his name.

If as a spiritual leader you get offended when someone doesn't use your title, you may need to examine your position. We are defined as leaders by our traits in the Kingdom, not by our titles in the church. Therefore, we should always answer to our name, and strive to always respond to our purpose. If someone addresses you by your name in a Church setting and it offends you, then there is a lack of humility and ungodly expectation of entitlement that needs to be addressed in the Spirit. You should be content with the fact that God knows your name. It is irrelevant who knows your title.

The time is now for us to choose our allegiance to God and our own spiritual well-being over our allegiance to pastors and churches. How will you know when it's time to leave? You will know because the Word you are receiving does not spring forth life, it does not edify, and it does not equip. You will know because you begin to attend out of obligation to man versus expectation from God. You will know because you literally leave service feeling lower than when you arrived. You will know because petty differences become misunderstandings and confrontations. You will know because you will end up with more questions than answers.

If you are in leadership and you are hearing from the Spirit of God that it's time for a shift, be respectful and have a phone call or face to face meeting with your spiritual leader. Let them know your time there is up. Thank them for what they have done and what they have sown into your life thus far. Tell them when your last day will be, even if immediately. If you are afraid to do this, that is a good indication that your relationship with your leader is misaligned with the will of God. You should never be afraid or have anxiety about approaching your spiritual leader.

Listen, there are some leaders who will try to strongarm you into staying. They will try to make you feel guilty and condemned. This is witchcraft. They are not operating under the influence of the True and Living God. There is not a single soul that Christ forced to follow him, they all followed him willingly. If a pastor tries to convince you that walking away from him, her, or their church equates to walking away from God, then you should know they are out of order. This is illegitimate authority. They are more concerned with losing numbers than losing souls. If they were concerned only for your soul, they would want you to be planted wherever you are most fruitful. They would be able to accept, with humility and meekness, that what is best for you and your family may not be them and their ministry.

Real leaders will not berate you, belittle you, or try to boss you. They will pray for you and release you. But know this, you simply cannot afford to stay in a church because you grew up there, or because you have a position there, or because you "think" you are needed there. You must go where God himself is sending you and put down roots where God himself has planted you. I implore you, those who believe in the True and Living God, to examine your place, your position, and your purpose. Ask the Holy Spirit if they are aligned according to God's will for your life. Are you growing? Are you being edified? Do you leave tired more often than you do refreshed? Are you working or are you worshiping? You can do both, but if you are not called to the Work that you are doing, then your Worship will suffer. Do you feel encouraged and empowered by your leader? Or do you feel burdened and obligated to your leader? If so, it's time for a shift.

There are so many whose gifts are sitting dormant in these churches because their leaders are insecure, intimidated, irresponsible, and inconsistent. Do not allow your purpose to be pimped, mishandled, abused, or misappropriated. First, make sure you are not the cause, and if it is time to go, go, but go correctly. Do not let your mouth be upon the man or woman of God no matter what you think you have a right to say. Seek God, allow him to speak to you, to lead and guide you into all truth, that your purpose, your position, and your place may line up.

God's voice is his Word. Pastors, Teachers, and Prophets are called to clarify that voice. When they speak, their words ought to confirm Gods Word. Do not allow any person or preacher to impose their personal convictions upon you as ordinances of God, rather try the

Spirit to see whether it be of God. How do we try the spirit? By searching out what you hear in the Word of God.

Your soul is too valuable to allow everyone and everything to have a say. The Lord will use people, but so will the devil! Even if what they are saying is Biblical, if spoken out of context or for the wrong reasons, it is equivalent to a false doctrine. God's Word is more than ancient scrolls selected and translated by a 17th century European king. It is more than a book of laws and commandments. It is more than prophecy, proverbs, and parables. It is understanding and empathy. It is love and compassion. It is also motive and intent. The devil quoted scripture to Jesus in the wilderness, he spoke the truth and yet Jesus rebuked him. Why? Because the devil did not speak truth to bring life, but instead to manipulate Jesus' purpose. Be careful of the vipers in the church; those who do not preach truth for life, but as a death wish meant to manipulate and obligate you without understanding.

Even when a Prophet speaks, he or she is not Foretelling, but Forthtelling, speaking that which God has already said concerning you. Even though you have not heard it in the flesh before, it should bear witness in your Spirit, because God is in constant communication with your Spirit. The "five-fold ministry" exists only to Clarify God's Voice. To make it plain, so that those who hear it can receive him, and those who receive him can run with endurance the race that is set before them. God removed the middleman when he sent his only begotten Son. Refuse to allow a title to stand between you and God, even if you're the one wearing it. Seek God in his Word consistently, so you will know what he is saying to you, about you. This way you can recognize and respond to his voice, regardless of the vessel he uses.

THE CHURCH AND THE SIDE CHICK

When we hear the term "Side Chick" we normally default to "the other woman". Some folks use this word loosely, but technically there can't be a side chick unless there is a wife. Except for his mother and daughters, all the women in a man's life are on an equal playing field unless there is a covenant in place. Until a man vows to be faithful and committed to one woman he is not obligated to be faithful and committed to any woman.

Once the commitment is official, the code of conduct between him and other women shifts to accommodate his vows. To step outside of that covenant for any reason is to dishonor himself and his wife. This is the foundation and picture I have in mind when I read Paul's letter to the Church at Corinth in 2 Corinthians 11:2–4:

> "For I am jealous for you with the jealousy of God himself. I promised you as a pure bride to one husband—Christ. But I fear that somehow your pure and undivided devotion to Christ will be corrupted, just as Eve was deceived by the cunning ways of the serpent. You happily put up with whatever anyone tells you, even if they preach a different Jesus than the one we preach, or a different kind of Spirit than the one you received, or a different kind of gospel than the one you believed.

The implication is that the "Bride" is the body of believers that make up the Ekklesia, or universal church. Paul is admonishing the church here for being distracted with a false image of Christ, a false presence of the Holy Spirit, and a "different kind of gospel" which is a false doctrine. Paul always seemed to be a bit gangsta to me. He's anointed at getting people told, and he doesn't disappoint as he continues in 2 Corinthians 11:4–5:

"But I don't consider myself inferior in any way to these "super apostles" who teach such things. I may be unskilled as a speaker, but I'm not lacking in knowledge. We have made this clear to you in every possible way."

In other words, Paul is saying I don't care who told you what. I don't care how long they've been saved. I don't care where they went to seminary. I don't care how many degrees they have. I don't care how big their church is. Ain't none of these "super saints" better than me, and although I might not be the best preacher out here, I have given you the truth. (Desimber International Version)

If the Apostle Paul were walking the earth today, he could write this same letter to the church and it would be accurate. The church has been tainted with all manner of man-made religion. Not only have these self-righteous pastors, preachers, and false prophets twisted the image of Christ to fit their own agendas, they have subjected his Bride to an illegitimate relationship with the Law. So now the Church, this "chaste virgin", has been forced into a theological ménage à trois with the first covenant of the Law and the second covenant of Grace.

They will use these inspiring messages of God's unconditional love to draw in the masses. They will tell you out of one side of their mouths that you have been saved by grace, the unmerited favor of God. Then once they get you into the building, out of the other side of their mouths they burden the believers with a battery of traditions to conform to, rituals to observe, and regulations to abide by that they barely honor themselves. Jesus addressed the matter in Matthew 23:1–4:

"Then Jesus spoke to the multitudes and to his disciples, saying: The scribes and the Pharisees sit in Moses' seat. Therefore whatever they tell you to observe, that observe and do, but do not do according to their works; for they say, and do not do. For they bind heavy burdens, hard to bear, and lay them on men's shoulders; but they themselves will not move them with one of their fingers."

These spiritual leaders have refused to divorce themselves from the concept of salvation through works and have instead chosen to cherry-pick certain laws to impose on the Body of Christ. Out of over 600 commandments that make up the Law of Moses, these pastors extract the ones that aid their agendas the most and preach them as a mandate from God. The problem is we can't afford to split time between grace and the Law. If we could manage to keep the Law consistently then what need would we have for a Savior? Paul tackles the issue again in a letter to the Church at Colossae in Colossians 2:13–15:

> "And you, being dead in your trespasses and the uncircumcision of your flesh, he has made alive together with him, having forgiven you all trespasses, having wiped out the handwriting of requirements that was against us, which was contrary to us. And he has taken it out of the way, having nailed it to the cross. Having disarmed principalities and powers, he made a public spectacle of them, triumphing over them in it."

This right here. This is the message of freedom muted by religion and legalism. This is the fullness of the miracle of Salvation. Once we were dead, and Christ has made us alive "together with him". He did this by wiping out the "handwriting of requirements" which is the Law that was against us. It was contrary to us, not because it was inadequate, insufficient, or irrelevant, but because we could neither attain nor retain the greatness of it within ourselves sufficiently enough to honor it.

The very existence of the Law was an indictment against us. The scarlet letter of a tainted bride. The Apostle Paul, perhaps more than any other, understood this and made it his business to free believers from the bondage of the Law and those who would subject them to it. He implored us in Colossians 2:16–18 not to let anyone judge us in food or drink, or regarding the observance of festivals and sabbaths. Yet, on any given Sunday you will find some pastor or preacher pontificating about our duties to organized religion, specifically badgering and guilting their congregations into showing up every Sunday with tithes and offerings in hand. Paul says by submitting ourselves to this reproduction of righteousness, to this knock-off version of faith, is to cheat ourselves of our reward, which is the unconditional love of God, gifted to us in the form of his son, Jesus Christ.

What these pastors don't seem to understand, or maybe they do and don't care … is that by imposing these regulations on the church, they have made the life, death, and resurrection of Christ of no effect. And at what cost? For what reason? Paul asked and answered this question in Colossians 2:20–23:

> "Therefore, if you died with Christ from the basic principles of the world, why, as though living in the world, do you subject yourselves to regulations—"Do not touch, do not taste, do not handle," which all concern things which perish with the using—according to the commandments and doctrines of men? These things indeed have an appearance of wisdom in self-imposed religion, false humility, and neglect of the body, but are of no value against the indulgence of the flesh."

As long as I've been in church, I have never heard a pastor preach from this text in Colossians. I'm convinced most pastors won't touch Colossians Chapter 2 because it is overflowing with liberty. Too many strongholds would be torn down that have been built up by the church. Too many eyes would be opened. Too many hearts would be healed from the weight of condemnation. Too many believers would be released from the captivity of self-righteousness. Too many souls would be delivered from the grip of witchcraft, manipulation, and doctrinal deception perpetrated across these pulpits. If the truth be told, too many would reject the church and receive Christ.

I live in a small town called Laurens, South Carolina. As small as it is, you can skip a rock down the street and hit six churches at every turn. I guarantee you I could step into any one of them and expect to hear a message about the tricks of the Enemy at some point. But what about the tricks of the Church? What about being assassinated from the pulpit? What about taking friendly fire from other members? What about those nice-nasty encounters with saints fluent in religion but illiterate in relationship? What about the classism, racism, bigotry, homophobia, and xenophobia? What about the drama, chaos, and confusion in the Body of Christ? On top of all this, they want to burden believers with the weight of the Law.

Organized religion has prostituted the church to the Law at the expense of the people. They preach the scriptures but exclude the Gospel. They have turned the love of God into propaganda and faith into fake news. As a result, so many believers have lost their way and so many lost can't find The Way. But praise be unto God who has given us his Word as a compass. We need only look to his Word to find our way back to him. Again, the Apostle Paul lends us a map for the journey in Galatians 5:1-6:

> "So Christ has truly set us free. Now make sure that you stay free, and don't get tied up again in slavery to the law. Listen! I, Paul, tell you this: If you are counting on circumcision to make you right with God, then Christ will be of no benefit to you. I'll say it again. If you are

trying to find favor with God by being circumcised, you must obey every regulation in the whole law of Moses. For if you are trying to make yourselves right with God by keeping the law, you have been cut off from Christ! You have fallen away from God's grace. But we who live by the Spirit eagerly wait to receive by faith the righteousness God has promised to us. For when we place our faith in Christ Jesus, there is no benefit in being circumcised or being uncircumcised. What is important is faith expressing itself in love." (NLT)

Read that again, I'll wait ... Did you see it? Did you hear it? If you listen in the Spirit, God is saying our futile attempts at righteousness mean nothing. As a matter of fact, the Scriptures say in Romans 3:10, "there are none righteous, no, not one." Righteousness is the promise God keeps to those who live by faith. Holiness is the mantle of his mercy. The Law, in its entirety, was crucified with Christ on the Cross. Any pastor that preaches any portion of it as a mandate from God has not heard from God. Any Christian whose faith does not manifest in love does not know Christ. Any church that attempts to manipulate the masses with behavior modification is not a House of the Most High God.

The Church was never in these buildings. It has always been in the heart of the believer. God wiped away the Law with the blood of the Son to remove any barrier between himself and his Church. John 3:16 are his vows to the Bride ... "For God so loved the world that he gave his only begotten Son, that whosoever believeth in him should not perish, but have everlasting life." No prerequisites. No behavior modifications. No strings attached.

This is the Good News. This is the Uncommon Gospel. This is the grace that offended the church over 2,000 years ago. This is the grace that offends the church today. This is the garment the church has always been too small to wear. This gown was custom-made for the

Bride of Christ, hand-crafted like a limited-edition Vera Wang. His love is a perfect fit for the least of these. His grace has left nothing, and no one uncovered.

Once again, God is proposing to the Bride. But he is not sending his Son. When Christ said "It is finished" on the cross, his work was done. He is sending The Kingdom to reach The Kingdom; those who will announce his invitation without alteration. And this time the church won't be at the wedding. Not because it didn't receive an invitation, but because it despises the Author … the Finisher of our faith, and everyone he had the audacity to compel. The church has rejected the Truth. So, if the truth be told … the Church can go to hell.

I remember you was conflicted.
Misusing your influence.
Sometimes I did the same.

KENDRICK LAMAR

CHAPTER 7
STRAIGHT OUTTA EGYPT

I WROTE THIS BOOK FOR THREE REASONS

1. To expose the principalities, powers, rulers of darkness and spiritual wickedness atwork in the Church

Imagine someone making a conspicuous entrance, and after gaining the attention of the room, loudly declaring, "I did not come to bring peace!" What do you think people would be thinking? Most likely everyone in the room would be automatically on the defense, expecting the worst and waiting to protect themselves from whatever this person had in mind.

This is exactly what Jesus did in Matthew 10:34–36, when he said "Do not think that I came to bring peace on earth. I did not come to bring peace but a sword. For I have come to set a man against his father, a daughter against her mother, and a daughter-in-law against her mother-in-law; and a man's enemies will be those of his own household." It is not that Jesus intended to bring division, but by virtue of bearing the truth, division would be a certain consequence. And so it is with this book. I do not intend to cause division, but that is the nature of the truth. It is the sword spoken of in Hebrews 4:12

that pierces between soul and spirit, joint and marrow, exposing the thoughts and intents of the heart. For too long we have given place to the spirit of the Antichrist. We have given deference to positions over purpose. We have given reverence to traditions over truth. We have elevated denominations over sound doctrine. And somewhere along the way we stopped wrestling against the principalities, powers, rulers of darkness and spiritual wickedness in high places and welcomed them into the church with open arms.

How did we get here? Why have we become so comfortable with the adversary? At what point did we relinquish our post as watchmen and surrender the gates? I wrote this book to confront the spirit of the Antichrist that is at work and on display in the Body of Christ by answering these questions.

2. To bring healing and deliverance to the broken, bitter, and bound in the Church through my personal testimony

Some may find my testimony shocking. But for so many others it is all too familiar. My experience as a Christian is not an outlier or one-off event. There are hundreds of thousands, if not millions of people who have walked away from the church, hurt and broken. So many of them have been verbally, physically, sexually, and spiritually abused but have been afraid or ashamed to speak up. I hope this book gives them permission to heal, freedom to speak, and strength to walk away from the institutions of religion that have held them captive. John 8:32 says, "You shall know the truth, and the truth shall make you free." It is the desire of my heart that sharing this truth, my truth, will empower others to share their truth, and by doing so expose the truth about the church universal. I believe shining light on the darkness of the church, uncovering the prevalent toxicity of church culture as I have personally experienced it, will not only bring a greater level of deliverance to my life, but open the flood gates of self-realization, vindication, and divine deliverance to the life of others.

3. To re-introduce the world to God and the Gospel through love, truth, and the Life of Christ

I wrote this book during a global pandemic. Over 250 million people have contracted the coronavirus, over 5,000,000 people have died from COVID-19, with more than 700,000 of those souls lost from the United States alone. At a time when the safest place to be was at home, the clear and present danger was not the virus itself, but our unwillingness to accept the power of its existence.

While the doors to the church were open, many of the buildings remained closed. And it is in this moment, when phones and laptops became the new sanctuaries, that the true nature of the church was exposed. Evangelical pastors of southern mega churches were breaking the law to gather by the thousands. Pastors of storefront churches who have failed to advance with time and technology were condemning virtual worship services. Religious church goers were claiming government orders to stay at home, practice social distancing, and wear masks are an attack on religious freedom. And all of this was happening while the world was watching.

As a pastor, I stood on the inside looking out, knowing beyond the shadow of a doubt that I would not come in if I weren't already there. The church has departed so far from the meaning and intent of the Gospel you can hardly call it the Church. There are people claiming to be Christians condemning other Christians to hell because of their political affiliations. Right now, as I write this book, many have made the president their God, and have substituted the Gospel with the ideology of their political party.

There are now Christians claiming to attend church services during a global pandemic is an act of faith, and should they die it would make them a modern-day martyr. Not only does this defy logic, but it's a direct contradiction of God's instructions in Romans 13:1–3 which states, "Let every soul be subject to the governing authorities. For there is no authority except from God, and the authorities that exist are appointed by God. Therefore, whoever resists the authority resists the ordinance of God, and those who resist will bring judgment on themselves."

People who are in a relationship with religion see no problem with skipping past Romans Chapter 13 where we are instructed to obey the law, straight to Hebrews 10 where we are instructed not to forsake the fellowship. They will isolate one scripture without proper context or consideration for the intent of God in order to validate a decision they've already made. I wrote this book because we need to understand the truth about God, and how very little he has to do with the religious institution of the church itself, but it is the heart of God to make the believer his Sanctuary.

Most importantly, I wrote this book because I had to. I can no longer sit by while my brothers and sisters are dying in the Body of Christ—dying emotionally, mentally, spiritually, and even physically, because we're so busy going to church, we haven't taken the time to *be* the church. Furthermore, I need the world to know that being "saved" does not equal being perfect. It is my heart's desire that believers walk victoriously in their faith, free from the bondage of guilt and condemnation in every area of their lives. And finally, that those struggling with their faith may be reintroduced to the true nature of

God, and in doing so receive the fullness of Grace, the depth of God's mercy, and the complete expanse of his love and salvation available through Christ Jesus.

THIS IS MY EXODUS

On March 15, 2012 I had an emergency C-Section. I had preeclampsia and it became a threat to my daughter's life for her to remain in the place she was conceived. At just 29 weeks she entered this earth by force. My womb was cut open and she was extracted from an environment where God intended for her to thrive, but the conditions of my body would not permit her to live. Unable to remain in the womb and unfit for the world, she was placed in an incubator and remained in NICU for 34 days.

I carried her for 29 weeks, but I did not give birth to her. I was never in labor. I never felt contractions. I never dilated. So, while I can take some credit for her existence, I can't take any credit for her arrival. The date and time of her entrance into the earth was scheduled by the physician. He listened to her heart. He studied her movement. He observed my vitals. He determined she was under duress. He extracted her from an environment that put her existence at risk. My daughter was born on March 15th into the hospital, but born again April 19th into the world.

I know you know where I'm going with this but go with me anyway. The Church is where I began but the condition of the Body has placed my purpose under duress. I've spent 15 years in an incubator preaching a Gospel I never fully believed ... until now. I've spent the last 15 years preaching a Grace I never fully received ... until now. God sees my heart. He knows how I move. He knows the Church cannot contain me. This is a scheduled extraction. The Church can take some credit for where I am, but only God can take the credit for Who I Am.

I have a scar where I was cut open. I have the evidence that it took place. And to this day, the entire site of the incision is numb. While I recovered from the procedure and am no longer in pain, the nerves closest to the cut will never be the same. This is the evidence my body endured and overcame a traumatic event. This is proof that I carried life, even if I didn't give birth to it.

As I make this exit from the church, I know it's going to leave a scar because the truth cuts deep. There are some who will be numb forever, who will cut me off, talk about me, and attempt to disqualify my relationship with God. Nevertheless, I know who I am. More importantly, I know whose I am.

I have been called to preach an Uncommon Gospel. I have been called to reach for those reaching for God. I have been called to step outside the building and shine the light in. I have been called to preach freedom to those in bondage to sin. I have been called to give direction to those seeking to change course. I have been called to be a beacon of light to those searching for The Source. I have been called to be salt and light. But I can't walk in where I've been and where I'm going at the same time.

On Sunday, December 6th, 2020 I stepped down from pastoring The Rock Worship Center in West Union, South Carolina. I cannot spend another day trapped in this position. I cannot spend another day shackled in religion. I cannot spend another day concealed by tradition. I left the Church, and this is the closest I've ever felt to God.

The "Institution" of Christianity does not represent me anymore ... possibly never did.

I'm done calling myself a Christian because it's not a label or identity that originated with Christ. Jesus never referred to himself or his followers as Christians. Why should I wear a label that was created by non-believers and used as a derisive epithet when Jesus walked the earth? Furthermore, too many Christians append that label to words, actions, and ideologies that are blatantly Antichristian. If anyone needs to call themselves a Christian to set themselves further apart than the grace of God already has, I understand. But as for me, to have my name in the Book of Life, to identify with Christ himself is enough. I feel no need to identify with Christians.

Christianity as an organized religion and the universal institution of the church have proven insufficient and woefully incapable of embodying the character of Christ. That label can neither define, contain, nor encompass the Messiah, and I know too much about him to believe I need to wear it.

I am finished with Christianity because I have too much faith in Christ. I am a believer in the Most High God, the King of Kings, and the Lord of Lords. Christ was enough for the Apostles who walked with him, and Christ is enough for me. Grace is my pulpit. The Word of God is my microphone. And the world is my congregation. This is my exodus.

ARTICLES CITED

Beuving, M. (2020, October 26). *The evicted church*. Creo Collective. https://www.creocollective.live/home/the-evicted-church

BGEA Staff. (2004, June 1). *What is the unpardonable sin? I am afraid I may have committed it.* Billy Graham Evangelistic Association. https://billygraham.org/answer/ what-is-the-unpardonable-sin-i-am-afraid-i-may-have-committed-it/

Contributors. (2019, December 31). *Millennials aren't skipping church, the Black Church is skipping us.* Black Youth Project. http://blackyouthproject.com/ millennials-arent-skipping-church-the-black-church-is-skipping-us/

DeYoung, K. (2019, August 5). *Should women preach in our churches?* The Gospel Coalition. https://www.thegospelcoalition.org/blogs/ kevin-deyoung/women-preach-churches/

Downen, R., Olsen, L., & Todesco, J. (2019, February 10). *Abuse of faith*. Houston Chronicle. https://www.houstonchronicle.com/news/ investigations/article/Southern-Baptist-sexual-abuse-spreads-as-leaders-13588038.php?

Earls, A. (2020, December 11). Mental health declines among americans, except weekly churchgoers. *Facts & Trends*. https://factsandtrends.net/2020/12/11/ mental-health-declines-among-americans-except-weekly-churchgoers/

Grace to You. (2019, November 8). *Does the Bible permit a woman to preach?* Youtube. https://www.youtube.com/watch?v=n8ncOf82ZJ0

Jones, J. M. (2019, April 18). *U.S. church membership down sharply in past two decades.* Gallup. https://news.gallup.com/poll/248837/church-membership-down-sharply-past-two-decades.aspxs affiliation

Mullis, D. (2018, October). *The invisible congregant: The church's relationship with mental illness.* Moravian Church. https://www.moravian.org/2018/10/the-invisible-congregant-the-churchs-relationship-with-mental-illness/

Oxford, Ed. "My quest to find the word 'homosexual' in the Bible". *Baptist News Global.* https://baptistnews.com/article/my-quest-to-find-the-word-homosexual-in-the-bible/#.YovvNS-B1B1

Pew Research Center. (2019, October 17). *In U.S., decline of Christianity continues at rapid pace.* https://www.pewforum.org/2019/10/17/in-u-s-decline-of-christianity-continues-at-rapid-pace/

Scott, E. (2020, August 3). *5 self-care practices for every area of your life.* Verywell Mind. https://www.verywellmind.com/self-care-strategies-overall-stress-reduction-3144729

Storms, S. (2019, October 22). *A response to John Macarthur and an appeal for common courtesy.* Sam Storms. https://www.samstorms.org/enjoying-god-blog/post/a-response-to-john-macarthur-and-an-appeal-for-common-courtesy

Taylor, M. (2019, March 5). *Three women from history who might change your thinking about women preaching.* Wycliffe College. https://www.wycliffecollege.ca/blog/3-women-history-who-might-change-your-thinking-about-women-preaching

Tchividjian, B. (2014, January 9). *Startling statistics: Child sexual abuse and what the church can begin doing about it.* Religion News Service. https://religionnews.com/2014/01/09/startling-statistics/

Torres, F. (2020, August). *What is posttraumatic stress disorder?* American Psychiatric Association. https://www.psychiatry.org/patients-families/ptsd/what-is-ptsd

Walker, M. (2020, April 1). *Why is church membership in a decline?* Christianity.Com. https://www.christianity.com/wiki/church/why-is-church-membership-in-a-decline.html

Williams, B. (2020, October 9). *P-Valley character analysis: Mercedes & Patrice Woodbine (mother-daughter dynamics).* WritefullysoBrittany (Blog). https://www.writefullysobrittany.com/cut-tvfilm-review/2020/10/8/p-valley-character-analysis-mercedes-amp-patrice-woodbine-mother-daughter-dynamics

World Health Organization. (2018, February 15). *Arsenic.* https://www.who.int/news-room/fact-sheets/detail/arsenic

Many voices. One message.

Quoir is a boutique publisher
with a singular message: Christ is all.
Venture beyond your boundaries to discover Christ
in ways you never thought possible.

For more information, please visit
www.quoir.com

www.ingramcontent.com/pod-product-compliance
Lightning Source LLC
Chambersburg PA
CBHW071408120626
46546CB00002B/855